HARD AMERICA
SOFT AMERICA

*To Donald & Dorothy Benedetti
with best wishes,
Michael Barone
Nixon Library
August 2004*

Also by Michael Barone

The New Americans: How the Melting Pot Can Work Again

Our Country: The Shaping of America from Roosevelt to Reagan

The Almanac of American Politics (as coauthor)

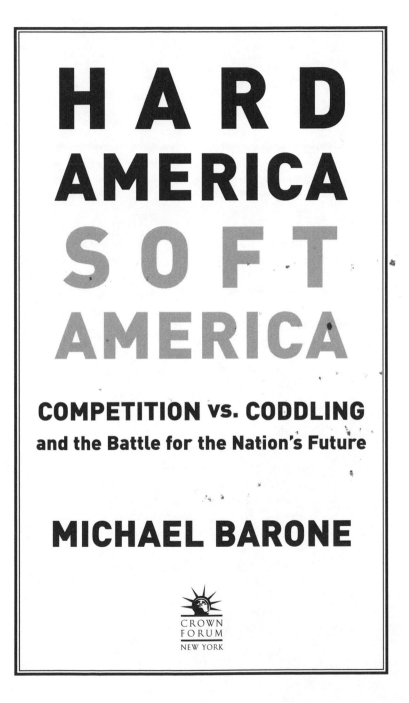

HARD AMERICA

SOFT

AMERICA

COMPETITION vs. CODDLING
and the Battle for the Nation's Future

MICHAEL BARONE

CROWN
FORUM
NEW YORK

Published by Crown Forum, New York, New York.
Member of the Crown Publishing Group, a division of
Random House, Inc.
www.crownpublishing.com

CROWN FORUM and the Crown Forum colophon are trademarks
of Random House, Inc.

Printed in the United States of America

Design by Leonard Henderson

Library of Congress Cataloging-in-Publication Data
Barone, Michael.
Hard America, Soft America : competition vs. coddling and the
battle for the nation's future / Michael Barone.
1. United States—Social policy. 2. Social values—United States.
3. Social ethics—United States. 4. Social rights—United States.
I. Title.
HN57.B332 2004
361.6'1'0973—dc22   2003023630

ISBN 1-4000-5306-4

10 9 8 7 6 5 4 3 2 1

First Edition

In memory of Daniel Patrick Moynihan
and
to Elizabeth B. Moynihan

CONTENTS

INTRODUCTION
HARD AMERICA AND SOFT AMERICA 11

CHAPTER 1
SOFTENING: FROM *SISTER CARRIE* TO *THE MAN IN
THE GRAY FLANNEL SUIT* 17

CHAPTER 2
SOFTENING AND HARDENING: FROM *THE LONG
GOODBYE* TO *THE GREENING OF AMERICA* 37

CHAPTER 3
HARDENING: FROM *RABBIT IS RICH*
TO *BARBARIANS AT THE GATE* 65

CHAPTER 4
HARDENING: FROM *MR. SAMMLER'S PLANET*
TO THE 2003 BLACKOUT 95

CHAPTER 5
HARDENING: FROM *IF I DIE IN A COMBAT ZONE*
TO THE IRAQ WAR 123

CONCLUSION
THE BATTLE FOR THE NATION'S FUTURE 143

CONTENTS

NOTES 163

ACKNOWLEDGMENTS 177

INDEX 181

HARD AMERICA
SOFT AMERICA

HARD AMERICA

AND SOFT AMERICA

Who was not impressed by the young men and women of the American armed services during the military action in Afghanistan and Iraq? Operating far from home, striking out into enemy territory more rapidly than soldiers ever have before, keeping vehicles and high-tech communications devices working in mountain wastes and desert sand, they won unexpectedly speedy victories and sustained exceedingly few casualties. They responded fiercely, with deadly force, to those who attacked them but also stayed their hand, at risk to themselves, when there was a risk of harming unoffending civilians. Soldiers on the ground communicated global positioning system (GPS) coordinates of targets in real time to pilots who responded almost instantly with precision strikes.

Thanks to embedded reporters and camera crews, we could watch these warriors in action and listen to them explain what they were doing. The young soldiers and sailors interviewed on TV spoke calmly, but tersely, in the awkward tone of adolescents; the officers, older and more experienced, were more articulate, but also plainspoken, terse, with confidence but not bravado. As I watched them, I could not help but reflect on how competent they were, how good they were at the dangerous tasks they had been given. They often, as they said, relied on their training, yet they also were able to adapt to new and frightening circumstances.

I could not help thinking also that only a few years earlier these enlisted men and women, and not so many years earlier these officers and noncommissioned officers, were more or less typical American adolescents. For many years I have thought it one of the peculiar features of our country that we seem to produce incompetent eighteen-year-olds but remarkably competent thirty-year-olds. Americans at eighteen have for many years scored lower on standardized tests than eighteen-year-olds in other advanced countries. Watch them on their first few days working at McDonald's or behind the counter of a chain drugstore, and it's obvious that they don't know how to make change or keep the line moving. They may have vast knowledge of the arcana of adolescent life, of certain forms of music and the characteristics of different athletic shoes, but they seem unready for adult endeavor, and not much interested anyway. This is perhaps an unduly harsh picture—of course, we all know of American adolescents who are remarkably knowledgeable and talented. And I have the sense that it was truer through much of the 1980s and 1990s than it is today. Yet there is something to it, as well. Half a century ago Americans leaving high school were expected to be ready to go out into the world and make their way. Today they aren't expected to be ready for that, and most of them aren't.

But by the time Americans are thirty, they are the most competent people in the world. They are part of the strongest and most vibrant private-sector economy. They produce scientific and technological advances of unmatched scope. They provide the world's best medical care. They man the strongest and most agile military the world has ever seen. And it's not just a few meritocrats on top: American talent runs wide and deep. Watch the software designer or the young doctor or nurse or the infantry soldier at work. Like a French waiter or an Italian artisan, these Americans know to do their work well and take pride in doing so. And, like so many men and women in the military, they often reach this level of competence well before turning thirty.

How do I explain this phenomenon? Because from ages six to eighteen Americans live mostly in what I call Soft America—the parts of our country where there is little competition and accountability. But from ages eighteen to thirty Americans live mostly in Hard America—the parts of American life subject to competition and accountability. Soft America coddles: our schools, seeking to instill self-esteem, ban tag and dodgeball, and promote just about anyone who shows up. Hard America plays for keeps: the private sector fires people when profits fall, and the military trains under live fire.

This book is about Hard America and Soft America. It is about schools and work, about the public sector and the private sector, about the economic marketplace and the marketplace of ideas, about the military and the universities. Unlike most of my other books, it is not primarily about politics: it is about how Americans live and learn and work, not about how they vote.

The book is also about how we have gotten to where we are today, and about where our society is headed—or should be headed. For no part of our society is all Hard or all Soft. Some people try to Soften zones of American life that seem too Hard, and others try to Harden zones that seem too Soft. Indeed, Soft America expanded during much of the twentieth century, as people sought to Soften an America that seemed overly harsh and unforgiving. Government regulation eased working conditions, and welfare state measures like Social Security provided a safety net for individuals. The Hard discipline of schools was eased by progressive educators. By the 1960s and 1970s, it seemed that Soft America might eradicate Hard America entirely. Proposals were advanced for government-guaranteed incomes, increased welfare payments, and more regulation of private-sector business; criminals were punished more leniently; even the military abandoned traditional tactics, procedures, and goals and suffered as a result. But in the 1980s and 1990s, Hard America fought back. Economic entrepreneurs and political innovators Hardened many parts of American life by their example and with their ideas. This Hard counteroffensive continues today, as we battle over how Hard and Soft the different parts of our society should be in the future.

Public schools, for example, may be the most notable example of a predominantly Soft institution—which helps explain why American children are confined mostly to Soft America. But as we will see, our schools have not always been so Soft; they have always contained corners of Hardness, and there are signs that they are getting Harder now. The private-sector economy, with its market competition, may be predominantly Hard, but it has always contained large niches of Softness (though many of those have been Hardened in the past two decades). Many public-sector bureaucracies are Soft, yet some have long-ingrained traditions of rigor and are therefore Hard, and bureaucrats' political masters are subject to the Hard discipline of elections.

So the boundary between Hard America and Soft America is not fixed. It is fluid, often moving back and forth. Most of us recognize that some amount of Hardness helps to maximize productivity and achievement. Yet most of us in our personal and professional lives seek zones of Softness in which we can go our own way. Adam Smith noted long ago that competing businessmen seldom meet without seeking to fix prices, to escape the Hardness of market competition with the Softness of assured profits.

I do not take the view that all Softness is bad. We don't want to subject kindergartners to the rigors of the Marine Corps or to leave old people helpless and uncared for.

Many Americans seek jobs in Soft America so that they will have time for raising their families and participating in community organizations, activities that provide American society with much of its strength and special character. It would be a cruel country that had no Soft niches. But it would be a weak and unproductive country that did not have enough Hardness. There will naturally be differences about how much of American life should be Hard and how much Soft—something reasonable Americans will argue about forever. But as we consider those arguments I think we have to keep this in mind: Soft America lives off the productivity, creativity, and competence of Hard America, and we have the luxury of keeping parts of our society Soft only if we keep enough of it Hard.

CHAPTER 1

SOFTENING:
FROM *SISTER CARRIE* TO
THE MAN IN THE GRAY
FLANNEL SUIT

At the beginning of Theodore Dreiser's novel *Sister Carrie*, published in 1900, eighteen-year-old Carrie Meeber is riding on a train from a small town to Chicago, with four dollars and a slip of paper with her sister's address in her purse. The city, as Dreiser describes it, is "a great sea of life and endeavor" stretching "for miles and miles in every direction." Indeed, Carrie arrives in a city that is growing rapidly; fifty thousand people move in each year, and new factories, railroad yards, department stores are sprouting up. But life is difficult. Her brother-in-law gets up at five-thirty every morning to walk to his job in the stockyards; her sister toils all day at child care and household tasks. To Carrie, who has never seen the city before, it is all strange: "Amid all the maze, uproar and novelty she felt cold reality taking her by the hand. No world of light and merriment. No round of amusement. Her sister carried with her most of the grimness of shift and toil." Carrie is expected to get a job and pay rent; the alternative is to fall into immorality: "When a girl leaves her home at eighteen, she does one of two things. Either she falls into saving hands and becomes better, or she rapidly assumes the cosmopolitan standard of virtue and becomes worse."[1]

This was Hard America. At eighteen you were on your own. School was long behind you: only 10 percent of young Americans went to high school.[2] Parents were relieved of any obligation to support you, or even keep you in their house. If you wanted to eat, you had to find work: Carrie's first job pays $3.50 a week. On the farm, where most Americans still lived, you depended on the year's harvest and fluctuating crop prices. In the rapidly growing big cities you lived bunched together: in many neighborhoods there were more people than rooms. One-quarter of urban Americans never married, as compared to just 8 percent today. Many men did not marry because they could not support a family[3]; they lived with their parents or as boarders in other people's houses and found sexual release with prostitutes.

Work was available, but difficult. Employers could dismiss you for any reason. If you were injured, there was no recourse: you could sue for damages, but courts usually found contributory negligence. The death of a breadwinner was disaster for a family, as Russell Baker shows in his moving memories of his mother's grinding hard work in the 1930s and 1940s. Yet there were bounteous rewards for those who succeeded. In a city like Chicago the contrast between rich and poor was stark. The rich paraded their wealth in gaudy mansions on city streets, in full view of passersby. Dreiser's Sister Carrie, on seeing the inside of a rich man's home, decides to leave her sister's apartment and assume the "cosmopolitan standard of virtue"; eventually she becomes a rich actress. Dreiser's book was considered scandalous because its heroine chose vice and was not shown to be punished.

Dreiser's grim vision of Hard America came to be widely shared. In the America that Alexis de Tocqueville described in *Democracy in America* in the 1830s, it was not considered cruel that people had to live off what they earned, that they were subject to the vagaries of the marketplace and faced disaster in case of illness or injury or death. The large majority of Americans were property owners who scratched out a living from their farms, and there seemed no way to protect them against such contingencies except through help from extended families and local charity. But in the booming cities of 1900, Hard America seemed to many unnecessarily cruel. And many feared that the urban masses, many of them recent immigrants from Europe, would rise in revolutions like those in Paris in 1789, 1830, 1848, and 1870. The rich in their mansions collected furniture once owned by

Marie Antoinette, proud to be able to live like royalty, but they must occasionally have had a frisson of fear that they might share the previous owner's fate.

The wealth that these people amassed was a product of Hard America. For years America's vast industrial expansion and surging economic growth in the late nineteenth and early twentieth centuries was taken for granted. The men who gained riches from it were referred to routinely as robber barons, the implication being that the rich were, in Theodore Roosevelt's words, "malefactors of great wealth,"[4] that they had unfairly grabbed the lion's share of America's growth for themselves. But there was nothing inevitable about that growth. It required the establishment of a legal framework—courts that enforced contracts, laws that permitted limited liability corporations. And it required investors who were willing to take enormous risks. Recent biographies—Ron Chernow's of John D. Rockefeller, Jean Strouse's of J. P. Morgan—portray these men not as robbers who took others' rightful gains away from them but as visionaries who created businesses and economic wealth that, but for their efforts, might not ever have existed. Rockefeller created new means of distribution and stimulated new uses for a product, oil, which had not had much economic worth when he started his business. Morgan facilitated a huge flow of investment in American enterprises by British capitalists who lacked confidence in other investment bankers. Federal Reserve Board chairman Alan Greenspan once playfully remarked that Morgan, who died in 1914, won World War II: if the capital investment in industrial plants that he fostered had not been made, the United States would not have had the capacity for mass production which was necessary for victory.

America's economic growth also owed much to an apostle of Hardness, Frederick W. Taylor. Taylor was the first efficiency expert, the originator of the time-and-motion study of how to perform every step of a job most efficiently. In the 1880s, Taylor, a rich Philadelphian, started working with machinists to make them work more efficiently. He gained a clientele of many factory owners and in a burst of publicity in 1910 and 1911 became famous across the United States and around the world. Taylor's work did promote efficiency: he conducted numerous studies to determine which kind of shovel was best suited to shoveling what he decided was the ideal weight of twenty-one and a half pounds per scoop of different kinds of materials. The result, he said, was scientific management, and for a generation or more Taylorism and scientific management meant more or less the same thing. But this engineering efficiency came at a human cost. "In the past the man has been first," Taylor said in 1911. "In the future the System must be first." As his biographer Robert Kanigel puts it, "His declared purpose was to take all control from the hands of the workman (whom he regularly compared to oxen and horses), and place it in the hands of management, yet he insisted that he aimed only to substitute 'hearty brotherly cooperation for contention and strife.' "[5] Taylorite management was Hard, with each worker held responsible for executing every move as the time-and-motion study prescribed, but it removed from the worker the Hard responsibility for the quality of his output: that was the responsibility only of management, which made all the decisions and did all the thinking. Taylorite management increased production, but at the cost of decreasing workers' autonomy and skills and removing their sense of accomplishment.

But even if the workplace was growing more unpleasant, American society was being improved in other ways. Rockefeller, Morgan, and Andrew Carnegie, who sold his steel company to a group headed by Morgan in 1901, also embarked on great philanthropies, well before the enactment of the estate tax. Rockefeller established the American system of medical research, Morgan developed great museums, and Carnegie built thousands of libraries. (Carnegie once told an importuner who was seeking money for a medical project, "That is Mr. Rockefeller's specialty. Go see him."[6]) These men felt a responsibility to use a large part of their wealth to benefit their fellow citizens, but they wanted to maintain the Hardness of America, which they believed was responsible for the country's great economic growth and creativity.

Others disagreed. From the new universities came voices for government action to Soften economic America. University of Wisconsin economist Richard Ely, trained as so many American academics were in Germany, attacked market economists and called for state action and trade unions. Also German-trained and also at Wisconsin, pioneering sociologist Edward Ross proclaimed that "sin evolves along with society" and that "tax-dodging is larceny, that railroad discrimination is treachery, that the factory labor of children is slavery, that deleterious adulteration is murder." At the University of Washington, J. Allen Smith explained that the ills of the cities were caused by "the self-ishness and greed of those who are the recognized leaders in commercial and industrial affairs."[7] Inspired by such academics, and responding to what they saw around them, Wisconsin and other states around 1900 started passing laws to alleviate working conditions.[8] (Wisconsin, with its university and its large German-American population, seemed particularly drawn to regulatory and bureaucratic remedies for social ills.) State legislatures started passing laws banning child labor, limiting work hours for women, and instituting workmen's compensation systems for injured workers. Sometimes the courts struck these down as violations of the right to make free contacts. Congress pitched in and in 1916 passed a ban on child labor on products sold in interstate commerce and established workmen's compensation on government contract jobs and an eight-hour day for railroad workers.[9] On the farm and in the small town, individuals did not seem in need of such protections: in a small homogeneous community neighbors were not likely to exploit one another. (Of course, white landowners were exploiting black sharecrop-pers in the South, but after the Civil War and Recon-struction most Americans put that out of mind.) But in the big cities, giant corporations employing thousands of workers in steel factories or small garment-makers pressed hard by vigorous competition could exploit workers with-out ever having to see them face-to-face. Individual ethics could not be counted on to Soften a necessarily Hard economic system; blanket protections, policed by disinterested bureaucracies, were needed to Soften an economically vibrant America which seemed Harder than it needed to be.

This Softening of America is usually portrayed as arising spontaneously in the political marketplace. But it was the product not of mass politics—the political bosses, who mobilized huge turnouts of voters, were often hostile to labor legislation, and the great urban masses spent most of their time working—but of intellectual elites. Such elites were purveyors of what historian Robert Wiebe calls "bureaucratic" ideas, "peculiarly suited to the fluidity and impersonality of an urban-industrial world. They pictured a society of ceaselessly interacting members and concentrated upon adjustments within it."[10] These Progressive-era reformers, the products of the new universities' faculties and professional middle classes, were eager to reform society in line with what they deemed to be scientific principles, seeking to impose a Softening order on the seeming disorder of the burgeoning marketplace of late-nineteenth-century Hard America.

One with great influence was the philosopher John Dewey. He left behind a mountain of difficult prose on all manner of subjects, but his greatest influence was on education. Dewey was a passionate egalitarian who disliked what he saw as the characteristic methods of American schools—rote memorization; book learning; a curriculum concentrating on English, history, mathematics, and science; testing and competition; teacher-led classrooms.[11] "Throughout his writings," Wiebe observes, "ran a limitless faith in the scientific method as the means for freeing people of all ages to learn through exploration and through social experience." Dewey himself wrote, "Education implies the guidance of behavior in harmony with social processes."[12] He believed that children growing up in farm communities learned partly through observation of the work and life around them, and he wanted children growing up in cities also to develop a working understanding of the processes that made urban civilization work. They would cook in the school kitchen, sew in the textile room, grow wheat in a dirt container in the back of another room. As his biographer Alan Ryan writes, "Dewey insisted over and over that school was itself part of life, not just a preparation for it, that the child had to bring into play at school all of his or her energies, not just intellectual ones and not just manual skills."[13] He founded a famous Laboratory School at the University of Chicago and inspired the creation of Teachers College at Columbia University. For Dewey it was not enough to teach children the lessons of the past; it was important to prepare them to deal with a rapidly changing society. "It is impossible to foretell definitely just what civilization will be 20 years from now," he wrote. "Hence it is impossible to prepare the child for any precise set of conditions."[14]

The Progressive movement of which Dewey was a part saw its political influence wane in the 1920s. But the move toward progressive education, inspired by Dewey's ideas, made gains in that decade and the next—though its advocates misinterpreted Dewey's ideas, as he himself protested in 1938.[15] Progressive education came to be the accepted dogma of the schools of education, state and federal education bureaus, city school boards, and professional education associations and would continue to be for decades. "By the 1940s," writes scholar Diane Ravitch, "the ideals and tenets of progressive education had become the dominant American pedagogy."[16] The advocates of progressive education argued, incorrectly, that the Hard science of psychology had proven that it was better to teach reading by getting children to recognize whole words than by phonics, and that the study of subjects like Latin and advanced mathematics did not improve mental discipline. The curriculum, they said, should concentrate not on traditional subjects but on "life activities"—language activities, health activities, leisure activities, vocational activities. Memorization and drill were bad; projects and "life experience" good. As Ravitch recounts, these progressive education advocates produced "a pronounced shift in the state goals of schooling, away from concern with intellectual development and mastery of subject matter to concern for social and emotional development and to the adoption of 'functional' objectives related to areas such as vocation, health and family life."[17] A well-publicized education manifesto published in 1944 proclaimed, "There is no aristocracy of 'subjects.' . . . Mathematics and mechanics, art and agriculture, history and homemaking are all peers."[18]

Thus was accomplished the Softening of an important part of American life. The champions of progressive education argued that it was more democratic than traditional education, because it included activities that could be mastered by any student. And enrollment did increase: while only 10 percent of high-school–aged children attended high school in 1900, 65 percent did by 1950.[19] But progressive education did not encourage upward mobility. The progressive educators, Ravitch writes, "saw their task to be one of fitting the children to the needs of the social order."[20] They took great satisfaction when schools reduced the percentage of students in college-preparation courses and discouraged blacks from learning trades in which they were thought unlikely to get jobs.[21] Traditional Hard schools provided a chance for children to achieve more than their parents had. Progressive Soft schools encouraged conformity and contentment with their lot.

In the 1920s and 1930s, progressive education continued its march through the schools. It did not prevail everywhere. Hard niches remained, especially in the academically elite public high schools of the big cities—New York, Boston, Philadelphia, Detroit, Chicago, San Francisco— which enabled the children of Jewish and other immigrants to work their way from poverty to intellectual excellence within one generation. Some teachers and principals resisted the progressive onslaught. But the progressive educators provided something which the earlier Hard tradition did not—a way to deal with the great masses of children pouring into the public schools who were not academically gifted. Parents and voters were mostly satisfied with what the self-proclaimed experts provided.

Meanwhile, suddenly, unexpectedly, another part of American life became dismayingly Harder. The private-sector economy had grown in bursts alternating with busts pretty dependably since the Civil War. But it expanded in an especially large burst in the 1920s and then went bust in the four years after the stock market crash of 1929. The dizzying collapse of the economy from 1929 to 1933 made America seem intolerably Hard. The gross domestic product declined by nearly 50 percent, and unemployment, in the days before unemployment insurance gave workers an incentive to report their joblessness, rose to 25 percent. International trade declined by 90 percent. The economy seemed caught in a downward spiral, and President Franklin Roosevelt's impulse was to encourage not growth but stability. The First New Deal—the National Recovery Administration (NRA), the Agricultural Adjustment Administration (AAA)—attempted to freeze wages and prices and to guarantee farmers' income. But in May 1935 the Supreme Court declared the NRA unconstitutional, aborting the first effort to create a Soft economic niche for Americans.

This led to the Second New Deal, which was of a different character, with economic redistribution (steeply progressive taxes) and measures providing Soft economic niches in the Progressive tradition. One provision was the Wagner Act, passed in July 1935, which guaranteed the right of labor unions to organize and gave them a privileged position as bargaining agents. This made possible the growth of giant CIO industrial unions, most prominently the United Steelworkers and United Auto Workers, which represented virtually all workers in those two giant industries by 1941. Auto and steel workers were far from the lowest-paid workers even before the CIO unions prevailed: anyone with an auto or steel job was much better off in the mid-1930s than many of his neighbors. But the workers were subject to the strict discipline of Taylorite time-and-motion studies.[22] And they were aware that if they failed to meet their required hourly quotas, they could be readily replaced: thousands of unemployed Americans would be happy to take their jobs, however exhausting and tedious the work. Union membership may have given them higher wages, but, even more important, it gave them protection against the Hard rigors of Taylorite discipline; it gave them a Soft niche.

Another major achievement of the New Deal was the Social Security Act, passed in August 1935. This promised old-age pensions for retired workers. It did not provide immediate aid (the first Social Security check did not go out until 1941) and was far from generous (the retirement age was set at sixty-five at a time when most American men were dead by that age). But it did Soften the economic system in a profound way. No longer would Americans have to set aside enough wealth to finance retirement, or be dependent on relatives or charity; now they would be guaranteed a minimal retirement income. Another section of the law provided monthly payments for single mothers with children—mostly widows, it was assumed,[23] people like Russell Baker's mother, who through no fault of their own were consigned to poverty by Hard America. The last major New Deal legislation was the Fair Labor Standards Act, passed in 1938, which established a national minimum wage of forty cents an hour, prohibited child labor, and established a maximum forty-hour workweek, with time-and-a-half for overtime. This was the culmination of the piecemeal Progressive-era laws on these subjects. Again, it was not an immediately generous law: it immediately raised the wages of only 750,000 workers, 1.4 percent of the workforce. But for the future it guaranteed a Softening of the Hard economic marketplace.

The consolidation of businesses in the first thirty years of the twentieth century, the economic legislation of the New Deal, and, most important, World War II created a Big Unit America—an America in which Big Business, Big Government, and Big Labor dominated the economic life of the nation.[24] Big Business was already well established before the 1930s, and during that decade large firms mostly avoided bankruptcy through stringent cutbacks and mostly avoided competition because potential competitors could not raise capital. Big Labor was largely a creation of New Deal legislation: union membership among non–farm workers rose from 6 percent in 1933 to 16 percent in 1940 and 27 percent in 1945; it would peak at 28 percent in 1954. World War II, by Franklin Roosevelt's decision, was waged by the triumvirate of Big Units. Roosevelt could have nationalized the railroads and the shipping industry, as Woodrow Wilson had in World War I (Roosevelt was familiar with this example: he was assistant secretary of the Navy then), or he could have had the government produce most weapons, as it had up to World War I. Instead he decided that Big Business would produce the weapons and brought Big Business executives in to help win the war effort. He could have refrained from encouraging the unionization of war industries, as Wilson had in World War I or a Republican president surely would have done in World War II. Instead he issued rules encouraging union membership and enlisted Big Labor leaders in an effort to prevent strikes and keep the assembly lines moving. He got cooperation from all of them except the United Mine Workers' crusty and isolationist John L. Lewis.

The war was a Hard test, and America passed. But the mass production that provided the tools of war and the military forces that won the battles did not perform as smoothly as we remember more than half a century later. Contemporaries complained about one bottleneck after another in war production, one snafu after another in military operations. There were massive inefficiencies and wastes of manpower. War produces a command economy, and a command economy, as we have come to know, is inevitably much less efficient than a market economy. The wonder is that the command economy was as efficient as it was and that the massive military, made up almost entirely of men with no military experience, was as effective as it was. Americans improvised their way around bottlenecks and adjusted for snafus. Undergirding their adaptability was a sense that things mattered: a war was on and everything you did could make a difference. In an April 1942 fireside chat President Roosevelt told of the exploits of B-17 pilot Hewitt Wheless from Menard, Texas, and the next month Wheless addressed eighteen thousand workers at a Boeing plant in Seattle, telling them, "The men operating the planes don't want all the credit. I want to thank you for myself and for a lot of other pilots who more or less

31

owe their lives to your design and workmanship. Continue the good work and together we can't lose."[25]

And so the war was won, with prodigious mass production and a military of 12 million men (in a nation of 140 million). The prestige that Big Units won from that victory endured for a generation after the war. As historian Derek Leebaert writes, "The future [after 1945] would belong to rigid, pyramidal organizations, whether of business or government."[26] And rigid, pyramidal organizations were inevitably full of many Soft niches. Advocates of the Big Unit economy, notably economist John Kenneth Galbraith, opined that Big Units were efficient because of economies of scale and the superior expertise of managers. But economies of scale go only so far, and the expertise of managers is often overstated. Large organizations tend to give tenure to most of their employees, especially when they are unionized. Why go through all the messiness of firing people when enormous amounts of money are gushing in? And like large ships, large organizations are hard to turn around in a short space. They find it hard to spur innovation within their ranks when current products and methods seem to be producing a lot for everyone. In looking at the post–World War II years, Leebaert nails the weakness of the Big Unit economy: "Absent significant foreign competition, all companies in an industry could labor under the same regime of government-imposed burdens and benefits. They found the visible hand of federal involvement surprisingly congenial. However, this vision of extolling the big and centralized government came expensively in terms of creativity and speed. The bigger an undertaking, the more likely it is to be wasteful: economies of scale are brought about only by conscious effort and competition."[27]

This was the era of the Organization Man, described in the 1956 book of that name by William H. Whyte,[28] and other-directedness, the term used by David Riesman in *The Lonely Crowd*. It was an era of conformity, when it seemed more important to get along with others than to make an original contribution. Whyte decried the tendency to see "the bureaucrat as hero" and for education to be increasingly vocational; he saw "the fundamental premise of the new model executive" as "be loyal to the company and the company will be loyal to you." A brilliant observer of everyday life, Whyte reported hearing again and again that all the great scientific advances had already been made and all that was left to do was to manage things; his chapter on scientific research in business, entitled "The Fight Against Genius," recounted how managers preferred scientists and engineers who could get along with one another over those with quirky personalities and original ideas. Organization men were being held accountable—but not for results: "togetherness" was the objective. Even contemporary fiction, Whyte thought, taught this lesson. "The vision of life presented in popular fare," he wrote, "has been one in which conflict has been slowly giving way to adjustment."[29] A case in point was *The Caine Mutiny*, a bestseller of the 1950s. In the book, the executive officer of the *Caine* replaces the incompetent and neurotic Captain Queeg when the captain refuses to head the ship into the wind in a typhoon. A court-martial results, and the executive officer is acquitted, but his lawyer turns on him, saying that he should have obeyed Queeg, his commanding officer, even though that would have resulted in disaster. The organization comes first.[30]

But that does not mean the organization in the ordinary course of things makes Hard demands. In the 1955 novel *The Man in the Gray Flannel Suit,* the hero works in an undemanding job and turns down a higher-paying position in which "you don't have any clear ladder to climb." He explains that he doesn't want to work too hard. "Of course," his boss says. "There are plenty of good positions where it's not necessary for a man to put in an unusual amount of work. Now it's just a matter of finding the right spot for you."[31] The admirers of the large corporations defended them not on the ground that they were disciplined by market competition but because they were run by men with managerial expertise. Big Business was balanced by the countervailing power of Big Labor, and Big Government exerted supervisory power over both. From the 1940s through the 1960s, presidents were deeply involved, and were expected to be deeply involved, in the negotiations between the coal, steel, and auto industries and the United Mine Workers, United Steelworkers, and United Auto Workers. It was understood that the wage and benefit packages agreed on would become the pattern for many other businesses, unionized or not. So ingrained was the expectation of government involvement that the new Labor Department building in Washington, built in the 1960s, had two large conference rooms adjacent to the secretary's office, one for management and one for union negotiators, so that the secretary could shuttle between them. Nego-

tiators justified their positions by citing profits and productivity, but in practice they were not held accountable in
the economic marketplace. Union leaders backed Democrats while almost all big corporation executives backed
Republicans; both groups believed or hoped that a president of their party would tilt the bargaining table toward
them, and sometimes a president did. But as it became
apparent that the economy would not return to depression, it became widely assumed that added costs could be
passed on to consumers, and they mostly were. The Big
Unit economy was inherently Soft.

America at midcentury was a far Softer country than it
had been in 1900. Security, a word seldom heard and a concept that seemed unrealistic in 1900, became a watchword.
The New Deal gave Americans Social Security, protection
against the Hard threat of economic disaster, and the
Softening in many other spheres likewise aimed to protect
Americans against hard realities. The benefits of this Softening of America were readily apparent. Who wanted to
return to the Chicago of *Sister Carrie* when you could live in
the Connecticut suburbs of *The Man in the Gray Flannel
Suit?* American health and living standards were vastly
improved, and millions who would have been ground
down by the Hard economy now lived protected by Soft
government programs. Schoolchildren who would have
been thrown out into the labor market by the academically
rigorous schools of 1900 were learning the skills of social
adjustment in the progressive schools of 1950, and getting
diplomas in the process.

The costs of the Softening of America were not as clear.

The surging growth of the private-sector economy after World War II suggested that you did not need a Hard economy to get production and plenty. Critics like Whyte could argue that the Softness of the corporate world was stifling creativity, but few people miss inventions that are not invented or efficiencies that are not realized. Progressive schools were producing young people who performed satisfactorily in the military of World War II and the Cold War and in the Big Unit economy and who participated more actively in voluntary associations and community activities—had more social connectedness, to use Robert Putnam's term[32]—than any generation before or after. Critics of progressive education became more vocal after World War II, but professional educators dismissed them as ill-informed or reactionary.[33] At midcentury some Americans were working for further Softening, through expansion of welfare-state protections, while some were working for some Hardening of the schools or the private-sector economy. But both projects seemed stalled in the 1950s and 1960s, when more Americans professed satisfaction with their institutions than ever would again[34] or, probably, ever had before (pollsters only started asking confidence questions in the 1950s, and it seems unlikely, despite what many analysts have assumed, that Americans always had similar levels of confidence in their institutions). But American society is not static. Over the next half century, different parts of American life would undergo waves of Hardening and Softening. And the process is surely not over.

CHAPTER 2

SOFTENING AND HARDENING: FROM *THE LONG GOODBYE* TO *THE GREENING OF AMERICA*

In the opening scene of Raymond Chandler's mystery *The Long Goodbye,* published in 1953, a drunk falls out of a Rolls-Royce Silver Wraith in the parking lot of a bar on Sunset Boulevard. He looks to Chandler's detective, Philip Marlowe, like a "nice young guy in a dinner jacket who had been spending too much money in a joint that exists for that purpose and no other."[1] Chandler does not explain what Marlowe is doing in the parking lot: this is not the kind of bar he would hang out in in the Marlowe mysteries published before World War II. The prewar Marlowe lived in a grubby garden apartment in Hollywood, a few blocks from his office on Cahuenga Boulevard; the postwar

Marlowe is installed in a comfortable house in the Hollywood Hills off Laurel Canyon Boulevard.[2] There were rich people in the Chandler mysteries of the 1930s and 1940s, but most characters were just scraping by. In *The Long Goodbye*, the characters seem to have too much money, to be corrupted by the riches so easily available in the Softer America of the 1950s.

Chandler was writing in the years when Los Angeles was America's fastest-growing metropolitan area, with new subdivisions, new shopping centers, and new schools going up every week. Superficially, this growth seemed to be the product of the Big Units. Big Government had located aircraft plants and shipbuilding yards in California during World War II and subsidized the West Coast's first steel mill. After the war, Big Business built auto assembly plants to serve the West Coast, and Big Labor represented their workers. But the growth began earlier. Even though 232,000 of California's 300,000 defense jobs vanished within a year of the war's end, in the next few years the Los Angeles area was generating one out of eight new jobs in the country and building one out of eleven of the country's new houses.[3] These new jobs were mostly the product of small operators, people who came to California in military service or to work at defense plants and who wanted to stay. As Jane Jacobs writes in *The Economy of Cities*, "The new enterprises started in corners of old loft buildings, in Quonset huts and in backyard garages. But they multiplied swiftly, mostly by the breakaway method. And many grew rapidly. They poured forth furnaces, sliding doors, mechanical saws, shoes, bathing suits, underwear, china, furniture, cameras, hand tools, hospital equipment, scientific instruments, engineering services, and hundreds of other things."[4] All this was going on in parts of the Los Angeles area that Raymond Chandler was not much interested in: a Hard private-sector economy growing even more robustly than the Softer Big Unit economy.

Also accelerating postwar economic growth were government programs that encouraged and rewarded upwardly mobile behavior: the G.I. Bill of Rights as well as Federal Housing Administration (FHA) and Veteran Affairs (VA) home mortgage guarantees. The G.I. Bill of Rights, the product of the American Legion and sponsored by the vitriolically racist Mississippi congressman John Rankin, provided educational benefits for veterans to attend college or obtain other training. At the G.I. Bill's peak, in April 1947, some 1.2 million veterans were enrolled in America's flabbergasted colleges and universities, which in 1940 had had a *total* enrollment of 1.5 million. (Little wonder, then, that the presidents of elite universities had opposed the program.) Almost 6.6 million World War II veterans, 46 percent of the total, applied for some training benefits by 1948; ultimately 7.8 million enrolled. The veterans were jammed into tiny classrooms; they lived in alternately frigid and steaming Quonset huts; they enjoyed little of the camaraderie or tomfoolery of the campus life celebrated by F. Scott Fitzgerald. But they learned. The benefits were generous. All tuition was paid, and single veterans received a subsistence allowance of $65 a month; married men, $90 a month. As a result, thousands of veterans who had never seriously considered entering college earned their degrees—and went on to make far more money than they had ever dreamed.[5]

Once they graduated they could afford to buy homes because of the VA home mortgage guarantee program. This built on the FHA program of the 1930s, which provided federal guarantees of home mortgages that met its conditions; the VA program was even more generous, requiring no down payment at all.[6] Many programs of the 1930s were Softening, protecting people against impoverishment or joblessness. The G.I. Bill and the FHA and VA mortgage programs were Hardening—they subsidized and rewarded only those who did something in return. Recipients had to attend college and graduate. They had to come up with a down payment or have served in the military, and then they had to make monthly mortgage payments. These programs helped to transform America from a nation in which most people did not graduate from high school to one in which most people attended college; from a nation in which most people rented housing to one in which most people owned their own homes. They helped to provide a Hard underpinning for Americans even as they were able to find more Soft niches.

And, of course, Americans faced Hard challenges on another front: postwar America quickly became Cold War America. By 1947 it was apparent that we were in a struggle with the Soviet Union; by 1949 it was clear that the Soviets had the atomic bomb and that China was Communist; by June 1950 American troops were fighting Communist troops in Korea. The military draft was reinstated and defense spending increased to levels far above those of the first postwar years. America's great strength in this struggle was technological superiority. "Never before had technology been so tied to national prestige," writes historian Derek Leebaert.[7] This was the country that had developed the atomic bomb, the country with the greatest array of scientists and engineers in the world. But that technological superiority suddenly seemed to vanish when the Soviets placed their satellite *Sputnik* in orbit in October 1957. It was known that both the United States and the Soviet Union were working to develop intercontinental ballistic missiles capable of delivering nuclear payloads. Now it seemed that the Soviet Union had developed a rocket with more thrust than any the United States had. This came as a shock at a time when a staple of comic strip humor were Soviet claims to have invented television and the airplane.

It also came at a time when there was increasing dissatisfaction with American schools, long dominated by advocates of progressive education. In the postwar years progressive ideas were deluged with a "tidal wave of criticism," in Diane Ravitch's words.[8] The rising percentage of young Americans attending college since the G.I. Bill of Rights went into effect made the progressives' emphasis on "life adjustment" and their distate for college prep courses seem poorly adapted to the actual needs of students and society. The prominence of former German scientists like Wernher von Braun in the U.S. rocket program—and the presence of German scientists on Soviet research teams— raised the question of why America was not producing such experts. Progressive educators discouraged the teaching of foreign languages, but the importance of understanding other societies seemed obvious at a time when American military forces were stationed around the globe and when America seemed threatened by people and events far from our shores. John Dewey had argued that education should help children be useful parts of society, but by the 1950s, progressive education had ceased to prepare children for the kind of society they lived in.

The launching of *Sputnik* made Americans suddenly demand a Hardening of their schools. Congress passed the National Defense Education Act in 1958 to provide funding for the study of mathematics, science, and foreign languages and for school construction and equipment. The National Science Foundation developed new curricula for mathematics and science. Former Harvard president James Conant's *The American High School Today*, published in 1959, called for larger high schools and for more rigorous academic training for college-bound students; it was a surprise bestseller.[9] America's decentralized public schools responded. Rural school districts were consolidated. More rigorous academic curricula were adopted. Advanced-placement courses were offered, allowing able students to study mathematics, science, and foreign languages earlier than previously.

These changes produced results. Scores on the Scholastic Aptitude Test (SAT) reached their peak in 1963, the year they were taken by the high-school class graduating in 1964. These were children born in 1946, the year that is usually taken as the start of the postwar baby boom; they were starting sixth grade when *Sputnik* was launched in 1957 and were thus the first class to attend junior high and high school entirely in the years of post-*Sputnik* Hardening. These children grew up to be the leaders of their generation in many ways. Presidents Bill Clinton and George W. Bush graduated from high school in 1964; Vice Presidents Dan Quayle and Al Gore and Senator Hillary Rodham Clinton graduated from high school a year later, in 1965. Children of this generation all had to compete on a Hard track from an early age, and they were hailed, while still in college, as the brightest generation in American history. These were the students who protested the draft and occupied campus buildings in the late 1960s and 1970s. *Time* magazine ran a cover story on the college class of 1968, calling these students "the most conscience-stricken, moralistic and, perhaps, the most promising graduates in U.S. academic history"; on the cover was Robert Reich, later Bill Clinton's secretary of labor. In 1969 *Life* magazine ran a story on student leaders featuring Hillary Rodham's commencement speech at Wellesley.[10]

Students at elite universities from the high-school classes of 1964 and the years just before and after rapidly made their way upward in American public life. Few paused to serve in the military, and many protested the Vietnam war; one who did serve in the military, John Kerry, became the spokesman for Vietnam Veterans Against the War and was lampooned in "Doonesbury" as a politically ambitious self-promoter in 1971, thirty-two years before he started to run for president. Strobe Talbott, a Rhodes scholar with Bill Clinton, gained fame as the translator of Nikita Khrushchev's memoirs. These students staffed the presidential campaigns of Eugene McCarthy in 1967–68 and George

McGovern in 1971–72; they started running for public office themselves in large numbers in 1974, a good year for liberal Democrats thanks to Watergate and a troubled economy. To them it seemed natural and unsurprising that they should be taking, at such a young age, a major part in politics and government. "This elite," writes *National Review* editor Rich Lowry of the group around Bill Clinton, "didn't just feel a call to run the country, it felt it deserved to run the country."[11]

About the wisdom of Softening America's economy these young people had no doubt; they assumed that those who had not excelled in the Hard schools they had attended needed Soft protection. They found it natural to support the expansion of Social Security, a project embarked on by a small group of dedicated professors and administrators active from the 1930s to the 1990s—Arthur Altmeyer, Wilbur Cohen, Robert Ball, Robert Myers. The idea was to expand the program incrementally, as political circumstances permitted, and to create it in a form that would be politically impossible to change.[12] The Social Security Act was passed in 1935, and benefits were increased and disability benefits made more generous in the 1950s. In 1965 Medicare was added, after a six-year political struggle. Social Security benefits were increased sharply in 1972, the result of something like a bidding war between House Ways and Means Committee chairman Wilbur Mills, who was running for president, and President Richard Nixon; the first increased checks went out on October 3, 1972, one month before the presidential election.

The launching of *Sputnik* was not the last Soviet achievement in space that shocked Americans. In April 1961, while the class of 1964 was in the last months of ninth grade, the Soviets launched a rocket that flung astronaut Yuri Gagarin into orbit around the earth.[13] This came during a season of embarrassments for the new American president, John Kennedy: the defeat of the exile force sent into Cuba's Bay of Pigs without promised American air support, the concession of Laos to the Communists, the imbroglio of United Nations forces in the Congo. Kennedy, who had been skeptical of manned space flight and who was warned against it by his science adviser, Jerome Wiesner, now took the view of his vice president, Lyndon Johnson, whom he had put in charge of the space program in January. On May 25, 1961, Kennedy made his famous pledge: "I believe that this nation should commit itself to achieving the goal, before this decade is out, of landing a man on the moon."[14] This was an audacious goal, one that would require vast increases in federal spending and technological advances no one could be sure of. And it was a Hard goal: it would be clear to all on December 31, 1969, whether it had been achieved. Franklin Roosevelt had set a similarly Hard goal on December 8, 1941, when he proclaimed, "The American people, in their righteous might, will win through to absolute victory." But he did not promise that that goal would be achieved by a time certain.

Kennedy's target date was met on July 20, 1969, when Neil Armstrong set foot on the moon and said, "That's one small step for man, one giant leap for mankind." As in World War II, this was a Big Unit victory; Big Business united with Big Government when NASA administrator James Webb, a veteran of the Truman administration, decided that most of the work would be done not by government employees but by private contractors.[15] Also as in World War II, a Hard challenge elicited superb performances by people who exceeded their own expectations and achieved an excellence of which they didn't think themselves capable.[16] Though mistakes were made along the way, they were recognized and corrected; difficulties were overcome by improvisation; obstacles were avoided by adept planning. Always the existence of a clear and unambiguous goal—a man on the moon by the end of the 1960s—sustained a sense of urgency and inspired extra effort. The course of the space program since 1969 has shown what happens when such a Hard goal is lacking. NASA has concentrated its money and psychic energy on the space shuttle program, a technologically underwhelming project whose cost has ballooned far above, and whose achievements have remained far below, expectations.[17] Two catastrophic and predictable accidents (Gregg Easterbrook predicted them in 1980,[18] before the first shuttle flight) occurred in 1986 and 2003. NASA has assumed that only government can develop space launch vehicles and has prevented private companies operating under the Hard discipline of the marketplace from developing them.[19] This is the product of a Big Unit program allowed to go Soft. (Interestingly, at least one private-sector initiative has tried to compete with the Soft government-run space program: in 1996 the nonprofit X-Prize Foundation, believing that "a small professional team could outperform a large, government-style effort," offered $10 million to the first privately funded group that successfully launched a manned spacecraft. The foundation's stated goal was to "jumpstart the space tourism industry through competition between the most talented entrepreneurs and rocket experts in the world," and as of the fall of 2003, more than twenty teams had registered to compete for the prize.[20])

The Hard space program's great achievement, in 1969, came at a time when the government had identified a new goal to be met: the elimination of poverty, urban decay, and other societal problems. As historian Walter McDougall observes, government leaders now hoped that the "Apollo method" might be the model for success; after all, "NASA had whipped the Soviets," so perhaps "technocracy—state-managed R&D, state regulation, state mobilization, and systems analysis—could be applied to 'down-to-earth' problems."[21] Those "down-to-earth" problems had become the focus of government, media, and university elites in the mid-1960s as a result of the success of the civil rights movement.

In the late 1950s and early 1960s, civil rights lawsuits and protests made news, and Congress did pass civil rights laws in 1957 and 1960, but in general politicians avoided civil rights issues as much as possible. Only reluctantly did President Eisenhower send in troops to enforce a school integration order in Little Rock in 1957, and political candidates avoided comments on the lunch-counter sit-ins and Freedom Riders (some of whom were violently beaten) in 1960. Indeed, politicians of both parties tried to ignore civil rights issues—Democrats because they believed they needed southern electoral votes to win the presidency and knew they needed southern votes to hold their majorities in Congress, and Republicans because they hoped to make gains among white southerners and were generally hostile to expanding the powers of the federal government, as any civil rights measure would do.

In the South, opinions were obdurate. White southerners almost unanimously supported racial segregation. To them it seemed unthinkable to alter the customary restrictions on blacks—calling adult blacks by their first names, for example, or requiring blacks to come to the back door of a home—or to end government-mandated segregation of schools and public accommodations.[22] Black southerners surely opposed this system, but most saw little reason to hope it could ever be changed. Whites outside the South had little knowledge of or interest in how blacks lived in the South and were not necessarily uncomfortable with local restrictions on the blacks who had been arriving since 1940 in large numbers in the great cities of the North. Residential segregation was the norm: in the 1950s, the newspapers in Detroit, where I grew up, had separate categories in classified ads for "Apartments—White" and "Apartments—Colored." When blacks began moving into a neighborhood, almost all whites proceeded quickly to move out. Northern blacks undoubtedly disliked the restrictions they suffered, but life in the North was freer than in the South.

One might conclude that blacks in the 1950s lived in Hard America, indeed the Hardest part of Hard America, but not in the sense that *Hard* is used in this book. It was a harsh America, an unfair America, an oppressive America, to be sure—an America full of unfair restrictions and unjust discrimination. But it was also an America where there was no reliable connection between effort and reward. In slaveholding America, in segregated America, in sharecropper America, blacks had no assurance of receiving fair recompense for their work and a fair measure of honor for their achievements. Even professional blacks, W. E. B. Du Bois's "talented tenth," made far lower incomes than whites of similar education and talent. There was little in the way of entrepreneurial tradition among blacks, little chance of getting loans from banks, little of the pooling of family and community resources to start businesses that could be found in many immigrant communities. Blacks were consigned to live in a Soft part of America, where there was little accountability—southern police did not do much to prevent crime among blacks—and little competition. Blacks were mostly barred from encountering the rigor of Hard America and from profiting from the achievements so often elicited by that rigor.

Historians of the future may wonder why white Americans in the North were for so long willing to turn away from the injustice of racial segregation in the South. But the fact is that there was relatively little travel between North and South in the years up to World War II, and relatively little moving across regional lines. From 1865 to 1940, millions of immigrants from Europe moved to the northern states, but probably not more than one million, black or white, moved from the South to the North, even though wages were twice as high in the North as in the South.[23] In the 1930s, sociologist John Dollard, a well-informed man, was

astonished by the formal and informal systems of racial segregation and racial subjugation he observed in Indianola,
Mississippi; the book in which he described what he
observed, *Caste and Class in a Southern Town,* was published
by an academic press, which suggests that Dollard's igno-
rance was widespread. Even in the 1950s, many in the
North were unaware of the extent of racial segregation in
the South: I can remember a classmate returning from a
spring trip to Florida and recounting with wonderment
and distaste the separate drinking fountains and restrooms
she had encountered.

It was part of the genius of Martin Luther King Jr. that he
saw that northerners would turn against southern segregation if they were forced to face head-on the unfairness of
the system and the brutality with which it was enforced.
Nonviolent protest, he thought, was the way to make all
Americans confront the realities of segregation. In May
1963 in Birmingham, Alabama, King persuaded hundreds
of schoolchildren to demonstrate peacefully against the
city's segregated lunch counters, restrooms, and drinking
fountains. Police commissioner Eugene "Bull" Connor
ordered that the young demonstrators be attacked with
police dogs and fire hoses. Local white leaders tried to
keep the TV film of this from being relayed to network
headquarters but failed. This was at the time when network
newscasts were starting to attract wide audiences; they
would be lengthened from fifteen minutes to half an hour
later in the year. The news footage had a profound impact
on national opinion. White northerners were suddenly
face-to-face with the reality of southern segregation and the

violent means used to enforce it, and they recoiled. In June, President Kennedy, speaking from his rocking chair and appearing on prime-time television, endorsed a national civil rights law banning segregation in public accommodations. His poll ratings in the South, where very few blacks were allowed to vote, fell. But they remained high and may even have risen in the North, and in 1964 virtually all northern members of Congress voted for the civil rights law. King's strategy worked.[24]

But in the process white Americans came to think worse of themselves even as they made the country—and themselves—better. If you had asked white Americans in 1961 whether blacks were treated unfairly in the United States, a very large number would have said no. If you had asked white Americans in 1969 the same question, a majority would have said yes—even though blacks at that point were treated much less unfairly than they had been eight years earlier.[25] Unfairness that most white Americans had been content to ignore in 1961 became by 1969 unfairness that many white Americans were determined to assuage and compensate for. And compensating for such injustice meant Softening many parts of American life—the criminal justice system, welfare programs, schooling, and more. This Softening was the response not just of a liberal elite but of the great bulk of the American people, who were determined to make up for the unfair and evil things that they had allowed to happen for too long.

The Softness of the response may not seem immediately obvious, and to many it was not obvious at the time. After all, police forces, National Guard troops, and, in a couple of cases, federal troops were called out to quell the riots of the second half of the 1960s—in New York in 1964, Los Angeles in 1965, Newark and Detroit in 1967, Washington and a dozen other cities in 1968.[26] But, in fact, these responses were measured, hesitant, less than total.

In July 1967 I was an intern in the office of the mayor of Detroit, and in the chaos of the riot I found myself in what we called the command center; at one point I was the only one present in a meeting between Mayor Jerome Cavanagh and Governor George Romney. Every evening as the sun went down after nine P.M.—this was the first summer since World War II that Michigan had daylight savings time— radio reports would crackle in of decisions to abandon one square mile of the city after another. The police were clearly not able to restore order; the mayor was hesitant to call in what he correctly regarded as the poorly trained National Guard; the governor was hesitant to ask President Lyndon Johnson to send in the much more competent federal troops; the president and Attorney General Ramsey Clark were understandably hesitant to take the unusual step of using federal troops to enforce local laws. Through all this ran an unspoken assumption that to send in too many troops was somehow a provocation, likely to create more resistance. The Detroit riot went on for six nights; eventually 2,700 federal troops coolly took things in hand. Careful escalation of force seemed the only course at the time.

But there were other options. In 1992, when blacks and others rioted in Los Angeles, Governor Pete Wilson and President George H. W. Bush announced within twelve hours that twenty-five thousand federal troops would be sent in. That riot lasted only eighteen hours. A Hard response worked much more effectively, and at much less loss in human lives, than a Soft response.

But a Soft response was what most Americans in the 1960s thought was right. Crime rates, low in the 1930s, 1940s, and 1950s, began to rise rapidly in the 1960s. In 1960 the number of violent and property crimes per 100,000 people was 1,126; in 1965, 1,516; in 1970, 2,747. In other words, the crime rate rose 35 percent in the first half of the decade and 81 percent in the second half—143 percent in the decade as a whole.[27] Nothing like that had been seen before in American history. At the time, many of us tried to dismiss the rise in crime as simply the reflection of more accurate statistics, which may have accounted for some of it but not very much.

And what was the response to this skyrocketing rate of crime? We put fewer people in prison. The prison population declined from 212,000 in 1960 to 210,000 in 1965 and to 196,000 in 1970. The low point was 1968, the fourth year of heavy rioting, with 187,000 people in prison.[28] This is extraordinary: many more crimes were being committed, but fewer people were put and kept in prison. This cannot be explained as the product of the actions of a small liberal elite. The American criminal justice system is decentralized. The number of prisoners at a given time is the product of the actions and decisions of hundreds of thousands, if not millions, of police officers, prosecutors, judges, jury members, parole and probation officers, and voters. By no means could all of these people in the 1960s be classified as liberals. No, a broad swathe of Americans who no longer felt morally justified in imposing Hard penalties on crime deliberately and substantially Softened the criminal justice system. And criminals increasingly were not being held accountable for their criminal acts. In large part this was a reaction to the melancholy fact that blacks committed a disproportionately large number of crimes: they accounted for about 10 to 12 percent of the population but appeared to commit nearly 50 percent of crimes.[29] But this Softening had devastating consequences. And the worst consequences, of course, were visited on those who lived in high-crime neighborhoods, most of them law-abiding black Americans; if blacks were disproportionately perpetrators of crime, they were also disproportionately crime victims.

Welfare was another area in which American society was Softened starting in the middle 1960s. In 1962 Michael Harrington, the longtime leader of the Socialist party, published *The Other America,* and the book attracted wide attention, especially in Washington when Dwight Macdonald favorably reviewed it in *The New Yorker* in January 1963. Harrington argued that many Americans—blacks in big cities and southern backwaters, poor whites in Appalachia, low-skill people stuck in dead-end jobs—were trapped in poverty, unable to escape.[30] He ignored the evidence, highlighted later by social scientist Charles Murray, that poverty declined steeply from the 1940s to the middle 1960s.[31] So after a long period of economic growth, poverty suddenly became more rather than less conspicuous; perhaps poverty is more noticeable when economic growth makes it seem avoidable.

The activist Kennedy administration took note and decided to do something about it. It had already passed a law to channel federal funds into Appalachia. Now Attorney General Robert Kennedy, trying to reduce juvenile delinquency, had come upon the idea that criminal behavior was stimulated by bad social conditions and could be reversed if people were empowered to change those conditions. Lyndon Johnson, eager for trademark programs of his own after he became president, announced in March 1964 his own "war on poverty." His legislation wove together many different programs, including a community action program in which poor people would fashion programs that would take them out of poverty.[32] At most times in American history it would have seemed counterintuitive to suppose that poor people would know how to get out of poverty; wouldn't people who had actually risen out of poverty themselves have a better idea? But in the civil rights movement Americans had seen victims of injustice instruct the rest of society on how to eliminate injustice. The idea of the poor leading the country to eliminate poverty seemed a natural analogy.

But while the civil rights movement had sought to allow blacks into Hard America, the new public policies actually confined more Americans, black and non-black, into a Soft America where poverty and crime were chronic. Those public policies included an increase in welfare payments, not only from Aid to Families with Dependent Children (the New Deal program aimed at widows with children) but also from the food stamps program and Medicaid. Under a 1968 Supreme Court decision, these welfare benefits could no longer be terminated if the woman recipient lived with a man. Under a 1969 Supreme Court decision, welfare benefits could not be limited to those who had been residents of a state for one year. Under a 1967 law, welfare checks were reduced for those with earnings by only one-third of the earnings. By 1970 the various welfare programs provided more economic benefits than a minimum-wage job. Welfare rights theorists urged eligible persons to apply for benefits and welfare workers to focus on maximizing the benefits paid out. As a result of all these trends, the welfare rolls grew rapidly in the late 1960s and the early 1970s.[33] Welfare dependency, like crime, approximately *tripled* in the ten years between 1965 and 1975 and remained at high levels until well into the 1990s.

Welfare dependency and crime built on each other. Welfare dependency meant that many children, including most black children, grew up fatherless at least for some period. Fatherless children, in turn, were much more likely than average to commit crimes if they were male and to go on welfare if they were female. As Charles Murray summarized in 1984, "The most compelling explanation for the marked shift in the fortunes of the poor is that they continued to respond, as they always had, to the world as they found it, but that we—meaning the un-poor and un-disadvantaged—had changed the rules of their world. Not of our world, just of theirs. The first effect of the new rules was to make it profitable for the poor to behave in the short term in ways that were destructive in the long term. Their second effect was to mask these long-term losses—to subsidize irretrievable mistakes. We tried to provide more for the poor and produced more poor. We tried to remove the barriers to escape from poverty, and inadvertently built a trap."[34] The great mass of well-meaning Americans who wanted a Softer response to crime and welfare dependency had in fact increased and perpetuated misery.

Another Soft policy instituted in these years was racial quotas and preferences. In the debate on the Civil Rights Act of 1964, Hubert Humphrey promised to eat the bill if it produced discrimination *in favor of* blacks. His reading of the bill was correct; it prohibits racial discrimination, and racial quotas and preferences are by definition racial discrimination. Yet in 1969 the federal government, trying to encourage more blacks to enter the building trades, specifically enacted racial quotas; they were applied to all federal contractors in 1970.[35] Quotas quickly became the norm in admissions to selective colleges, universities, and graduate schools. Strict racial quotas were banned by the Supreme Court in 1978 in the *Bakke* case, but the justice who provided the fifth and deciding vote also said that schools might be able to use racial preferences to increase the diversity of their student body—a portion of his opinion no other justice joined.[36]

Racial quotas and preferences are a Soft system: blacks and members of other preferred groups are not being held accountable to the same standards as others. Not being held accountable, they do not achieve as much. John McWhorter, who is black and is now a linguistics professor at Berkeley, remembers that in high school he "quite deliberately refrained from working to my highest potential because I knew I would be accepted to top universities without doing so." He goes on: "Imagine telling a Martian who expressed an interest in American education policy: 'We allow whites in only if they have a GPA of 3.7 and an SAT score of 1300 or above. We let blacks in with a GPA of 3.0 and an SAT of 900. Now, what we have been pondering for years is why black students continue to submit higher grades and scores than this so rarely.' Well, mercy me—what a perplexing problem!"[37] Recent studies have shown that black and Latino students do better on tests when the results determine whether students graduate.[38] It is notorious that high percentages of blacks and Latino students admitted to schools as a result of racial preferences fail to graduate. While university administrators preen themselves on their generosity, the purported beneficiaries of that generosity are often not well served by it.

In 2003 the Supreme Court addressed the question of racial quotas and preferences in university admissions for the first time in twenty-five years. In the *Grutter* case, the court allowed racial quotas and preferences for "diversity" but warned that they might not be permissible twenty-five years later. We cannot know what achievements by blacks and Latinos have been prevented from occurring in the quarter century from *Bakke* to *Grutter* and will be prevented in the quarter century after *Grutter*, but we can be sure that the purported beneficiaries of these quotas and preferences—and the larger society—have suffered and will suffer some loss. In this important part of American life, blacks will continue to be fenced off from Hard America and encouraged to live in a Soft America where lack of achievement will nonetheless be rewarded. Fortunately, many black Americans decline the invitation and advance and prosper in Hard America.

The success of the civil rights movement and the changes in attitudes it prompted also had its effect on education. The public schools of the early 1960s had been Hardened by a nation convinced that it needed rigorous education to produce the scientists and other experts it needed to win the Cold War. By the mid-1960s, the focus had changed. As Diane Ravitch puts it, "The pursuit of excellence was overshadowed by concern about the needs of the disadvantaged. As the racial crisis and the urban crisis became the nation's most pressing problems, the Cold War competition with the Soviets moved to the back burner and lost its motivating power. Identifying the gifted and stimulating high achievement paled as a national goal in comparison to the urgency of redressing racial injustice. Government agencies and foundations redirected their agendas to search for mechanisms to meet the needs of disadvantaged minority children, and scores of compensatory programs were created throughout the country. Such efforts were multiplied by congressional passage of the Elementary and Secondary Education Act of 1965, with its focus on educating poor children."[39] Hard schools were increasingly seen as destructively regimenting poor children. There were calls for "open schools" and "free schools." In the late 1960s, Joseph Featherstone of the *New Republic* wrote of English infant schools which seemed chaotic but in which teachers seemed to be gently nurturing learning, and his portrayals prompted American imitators. But many of the American schools that attempted to follow this model were, as Featherstone himself admitted, "a shambles." The Hardening of the schools in the late 1950s and early 1960s proved temporary and was followed by a general Softening, a process that ignored the progressive education experience and was based on one free-spirited theory after another.[40] Not surprisingly, academic achievement suffered. Test scores declined and remained at levels well below those of the early 1960s.[41]

All of these efforts to Soften life for black Americans, and for Americans in general, were misguided. For blacks in particular, the supposed solutions offered only exacerbated problems. The problem blacks faced was not that American society was too Hard for them, that they suffered from too much competition and were being held too accountable. The problem was that they were shut out of Hard America altogether, unable to reap the rewards available in a Hard system for those who achieve. The Softening of American society that started in the mid-1960s—the Softening of criminal justice, welfare, racial quotas and preferences, and education—had the effect of confining most blacks to Soft America. They were left unprotected against crime, deterred from forming stable families, deincentivized to achieve. The advocates of Softening hated the idea of imposing middle-class mores on black Americans, but middle-class mores are necessary for achievement in Hard America, and underclass behavior makes such achievement impossible.

Despite the problems that such Softening was creating, America was growing ever more Soft. In fact, at this time the idea that society needed any Hardness at all was being challenged. The challenger was Charles Reich, a professor at Yale Law School, and the challenge was issued in his bestselling book *The Greening of America,* published in 1970, when Bill and Hillary Rodham Clinton and many other members of the high-school classes of 1964 and 1965 were students at Yale Law. The book was dedicated to "the students at Yale who made this book possible, and for their generation": Reich, nearly two decades older, was appointing himself their spokesman. Reich portrayed America— the most prosperous nation in the world, and newly rid of legally enforced racial segregation—as "one vast, terrifying anti-community." He also lamented the dominance of Big Units: "Most governmental power has shifted from Congress to administrative agencies, and corporate power is free to ignore both stockholders and consumers." There was "a universal sense of powerlessness," even though solutions to every problem were obvious. "We know what causes crime and social disorder, and what can be done to eliminate those causes. [Later he identifies some solutions: "education, housing, and jobs."] We know the steps that can be taken to create greater economic equality. We are in possession of techniques to fashion and preserve more livable cities and environments." Taken for granted in all this is the productivity of the American economy.[42]

The problem with America in 1970, Reich wrote, was that most Americans had the wrong "consciousness," the wrong values and the wrong perspective in which to understand the society around them. Many Americans were still stuck in history, in Consciousness I, "the traditional outlook of the American farmer, small businessman, and worker who is trying to get ahead." Not that this was all bad: Consciousness I at least had "more humanistic values" than Consciousness II, which "represents the values of an organizational society." But both were bad: "This combination of an anachronistic consciousness [I] characterized by myth, and an inhuman consciousness [II] dominated by the machine-rationality of the Corporate State, have, between them, proved utterly unable to manage, guide, or control the immense apparatus of technology and organization that America has built."[43] What would transform this dreadful reality? Consciousness III, which is, simply, "the new generation"—or the part of it Reich had come to know at Yale Law School. It is "based on the present state of technology, and could not have arisen without it. And it represents a higher, transcendent form of reason."[44] It was spreading out from elite campuses to "wider and wider segments of youth," and it was irreversible.[45] The results would be wonderful: "The new way of life proposes a concept of work in which quality, dedication, and excellence are preserved, but work is nonalienated, is the free choice of each person, is integrated into a full and satisfying life, and expresses and affirms each individual being. The new way of life makes possible and necessary a culture that is nonartificial and nonalienated, a form of community in which love, respect, and a mutual search for wisdom replace the competition and separation of the past, and a liberation of each individual in which he is enabled to grow to the highest possibilities of the human spirit."[46]

This heady utopianism goes on for hundreds of pages and was widely regarded as a revelation when it first appeared. What it amounts to is this: America should become an entirely Soft society, and then everything will be perfect. Reich did his part: he gave all his students A's and soon enough left law teaching altogether and moved to San Francisco. Markets didn't work; organizations ruined everything; self-expression would produce a perfect America. No market incentives, no organizational rules, nothing but the indulgence of one's personal desires would produce a society in which all would have plenty and everybody would get along. It did not occur to Reich that the greening of America might be more like the corrupt louche Los Angeles of *The Long Goodbye*.

CHAPTER 3

HARDENING:
FROM *RABBIT IS RICH TO*
BARBARIANS AT THE GATE

I n *Rabbit Is Rich,* the third of John Updike's four novels
about Harry "Rabbit" Angstrom, the eponymous hero
is selling cars at the dealership he has (partially) inher-
ited from his father-in-law. But the cars he is selling are no
longer the long, low, chrome-laden Buicks his father-in-law
sold when the first of the *Rabbit* novels was published two
decades before. The cars are Toyotas, made in Japan—and
a good thing, too, because the year is 1979, gas prices have
shot up to $1.50 a gallon, and, for the second time in six
years, gas lines have become a part of daily life. An era of
scarcity and shortages seems at hand. "I figure the oil's
going to run out about the same time I do, the year two

thousand," Rabbit tells one of the other salesmen in a down moment. "Seems funny to say it, but I'm glad I lived when I did. These kids coming up, they'll be living on table scraps. We had the meal."

But there are cars to be sold. A customer drives in in a 1971 Ford Custom Squire station wagon—one of Detroit's behemoths. Rabbit quickly explains that the Toyota Corolla "will give you highway mileage up to 40 a gallon and 20 to 25 city driving" and is "much better than average on maintenance and repairs through the first four years." The time frame is deliberate: "That old Kleenex mentality of trade it in every two years is gone with the wind." And the Big Three automakers have not kept up. "If you ask me, Detroit's let us all down, 200 million of us. I'd much rather handle native American cars but between the three of us they're junk. They're cardboard. They're pretend."[1]

For many years the Big Three auto companies had been America's industrial giants, seemingly able to control the American auto market, coolly manipulating consumers into buying their cars every two or three years with flashy styling, clever advertising, and planned obsolescence (so that a three-year-old car would start to fall apart). But these techniques were no longer working. Rabbit Angstrom, on Route 111 in Brewer, Pennsylvania, may have been adapting, but the Big Three auto companies, and the American economy, were in trouble.

This was something that Charles Reich had not anticipated a decade before. He took as a given that the American economy would continue to grow. In this Reich was not alone. Even those who did not embrace his prescription for a new "consciousness" agreed that the problem of maintaining low-inflation economic growth indefinitely had been solved. The important question, therefore, was not production of wealth but distribution of wealth. There was no need for a Hard economic system. The economy could be allowed to grow Softer and Softer; indeed, in the natural course of things it must grow Softer and Softer.

This was the gospel taught in John Kenneth Galbraith's *The New Industrial State*, first published in 1968. According to Galbraith, the Big Units would continue to propel the American economy indefinitely. While Big Business was the dominating force, it was disciplined not by the Hard market but by the Soft countervailing power of Big Government and Big Labor. The U.S. economic system, "whatever its formal ideological billing," had become "in substantial part a planned economy." Large corporations would continue to gobble up most of the American economy, so everything besides the five hundred or six hundred biggest firms could be ignored: "To understand the rest of the economy is to understand only that part which is diminishing in relative extent and which is most nearly static." Corporate executives could create demand for all the goods they produced by advertising: consumers would buy what they were told they would like. And that made it easy for Big Business to negotiate with Big Labor, since the cost of any wage and benefit increases could be passed along to consumers. Only large corporations had the capital to afford expensive machines and sophisticated technology, so competitors were unlikely to arise. Meanwhile, Big Government, not Big Business, would produce the bulk of technological development—Galbraith had in mind military and space research.[2]

Like many prophets, Galbraith did a better job of describing the recent past than of forecasting the near future. He was describing the Big Unit economy which had done so much to win World War II and to build prosperous postwar America. And in the two decades before the publication of his book, Big Business had in fact grown ever bigger. The share of corporate assets owned by the two hundred largest industrial companies rose steadily from 47 percent in 1947 to 61 percent in 1968. The 1950s and 1960s saw little turnover in the top industrial companies.[3] Such companies, especially the Big Three automakers, seemed well insulated against competition and accountability; they inhabited what David Halberstam has described as "a protected world," with "the shares of the market already apportioned."[4] They generated enough income to finance expansion internally, so they did not have to rely much on financial markets to raise capital. At the same time, financial markets assumed that the large corporations' advantages of economies of scale were so great that domestic competitors were not worth financing.

So Galbraith was right in seeing corporate America as in some important ways Soft and impervious to market cues. But he was wrong in suggesting that that state of affairs would continue indefinitely, that the trend to Bigness would continue. He also was overly confident in the ability of Keynesian economics to sustain low-inflation economic growth.

By the 1970s, the Big Units were faltering. Big Government was supposed to produce low-inflation economic growth, but there was a recession in 1970 (the same year that Charles Reich published *The Greening of America*) and then again in 1973–74. President Richard Nixon imposed wage and price controls in 1971, but of course these did not reduce inflation; trying to abolish the Hard communication provided by market prices just made things worse. In fact, by 1979 there was both recession and double-digit inflation: stagflation, a condition which standard Keynesians had said was impossible. Big Business performed no better. The American auto industry, mentioned often by Galbraith, fell on hard times. As David Halberstam has observed, even while economies of scale made it difficult for competitors to the Big Three auto companies to arise domestically, German and Japanese firms started entering the U.S. market in the late 1960s. And the American automakers, so accustomed to their Soft, protected world, were not prepared to respond to competition; indeed, they did not even consider that competition could threaten their way of doing business. In 1970, after foreign competitors had emerged in the U.S. market, the auto companies reacted to a United Auto Workers (UAW) strike against General Motors by granting a generous wage increase; they assumed that they could make consumers absorb the cost, that styling and advertising would enable them to sell as many cars as they wanted, as Galbraith taught. Some, like reporter William Serrin, even argued that the UAW should have held out for more, that the companies could pay anything. "It is vacuous to think that the [Big Three auto] corporations will become extinct," Serrin wrote in 1974.[5] But over the next fifteen years each of the Big Three would find itself on the brink of bankruptcy.

Softness fostered insular habits of mind. What had worked in the past would work in the future. In innovation there was danger and risk. In 1973 a consultant urged Elliott Estes, then about to become president of General Motors, to start building front-wheel-drive vehicles. Estes nixed the idea, saying, "When I was at Oldsmobile, there was something I learned there that I've never forgotten. There was an old guy there who was an engineer, and he had been at GM a long time, and he gave me some advice. He told me, whatever you do, don't let GM do it first."[6] Then there was the matter of auto clocks. The electric clocks the Big Three installed in cars starting in the 1950s would stop keeping accurate time after the car owners manually adjusted them when Daylight Savings Time began or ended. But all the top Big Three auto executives lived and vacationed in Michigan, which from World War II until 1967 did not observe Daylight Savings Time; they didn't catch on to the problem for years. Experience also conditioned these executives to keep producing large, high-profit cars and to resist building smaller cars. After all, didn't every man have to have a big car to take his family up north in the summer? They found it hard to imagine that an increasing number of car buyers did not have families and did not take family vacations up north every year.

As Halberstam writes, "The larger the American industry (steel, auto), the less prepared it was for economic rivalry."[7] In their Soft niches, the men who ran large corporations lost sight of the need for quality and, as William H. Whyte saw, technological advance. They found that they could not command consumers to buy their products and could not pass along high labor costs without limit. Businessmen, as Adam Smith wrote long ago, prefer the Soft security of price-fixing to the Hard competition of the market, and people who work in large organizations prefer the Soft comforts of routine to the Hard work of innovation. But such security and comforts could not be guaranteed indefinitely. In the years after John Kenneth Galbraith wrote, the giant corporations, which held such seemingly stable places in the American economy, were buffeted by waves of competition. The rate at which companies left the Fortune 500 quadrupled between 1970 and 1990. In 1974 the hundred largest industrial corporations accounted for 36 percent of gross domestic product; the figure in 1998 had fallen to 17 percent. Their share of the nation's work force and corporate assets also fell by half.[8] As John Micklethwait and Adrian Wooldridge of the *Economist* write, "Big firms grew (by 1999, the average revenue of the top 50 companies in America reached $51 billion); they just grew much more slowly than small ones, which supplied most of the new jobs throughout the developed world. Big firms were much more likely than ever to go out of business by 2000; roughly half the biggest 100 industrial firms in 1974 had disappeared through takeovers or bankruptcy."[9] The relative decline of Big Business was most visible in manufacturing, notably in autos and steel, but it was also apparent in other fields, like retailing. In 1973 Sears was America's greatest merchant, proud enough of its standing to build the world's highest skyscraper in Chicago. By 2001 it had closed most of its stores, moved its headquarters to a non-descript building in the suburb of Schaumburg, Illinois, and spent years struggling to come up with a strategy that would ensure its survival.[10]

The sputtering performance of Big Business was matched by the sputtering performance of Big Government. One Hard underpinning of the American private-sector economy in the years after World War II was the government's guarantee of the dollar's convertibility into gold—its commitment to buy or sell gold at $35 an ounce. This made the dollar the linchpin of the world monetary system, and it enabled successive administrations and the Federal Reserve to wring out the inflation that was the inevitable result of wartime spending and of the wage and price controls imposed during World War II and the Korean War. During most of the 1950s and 1960s, the American economy enjoyed low-inflation economic growth sustained over longer periods than had ever been achieved before World War II. From this apparent policy success most economists drew the conclusion that Keynesian economic techniques enabled policymakers, using the tools of fiscal policy (federal budget surpluses and deficits) and monetary policy (interest rates as guided by the Federal Reserve), to achieve low-inflation economic growth more or less indefinitely. This was the lesson taught when I took Economics 1, the most popular course in the university, at Harvard in 1964.

But Keynes, as it turned out, did not have all the answers. In his writings he addressed primarily the problem of low demand and deflation—the problems that afflicted the

American, British, and European economies in the 1930s. Still, he knew there were other problems: few economists have described more vividly the horrific effects of inflation. And Keynes worked hard to prevent them: he played a key role in setting up the International Monetary Fund.[11] But that monetary system was abandoned in August 1971, when Richard Nixon came down from Camp David after a meeting with his economic advisers and announced that the United States would no longer sell gold to other central banks at $35 an ounce—thus separating the dollar from the gold standard. To prevent inflation, Nixon also announced a ninety-day freeze on wages and prices and ordered a study of what controls would be imposed afterward. (The wage and price controls were possible only because Democrats in Congress had passed a bill authorizing them—as a political ploy: they had expected Nixon to refuse to impose controls and planned to campaign against him for that in 1972. The need for controls was by no means obvious. In the year Nixon acted, inflation was 4.4 percent, down from 6 percent a year earlier; economic growth was 2.8 percent. Nixon imposed the controls presumably out of a fear that inflation would result from the devaluation of the dollar.[12])

President Nixon's new policies only further Softened the economic system. While hard money imposes a discipline on everyone (individuals, firms, labor unions, even governments), soft money weakens discipline and imposes costs: debtors pay back in depreciated dollars, creditors demand premiums to lend, and uncertainty builds inefficiency into the economy. Likewise, wage and price controls, far from

Hardening the economy, Soften it. In wartime they can be reasonably effective, for there is a stigma attached to cheating. But in peacetime—and America in 1971, with the number of U.S. troops in Vietnam declining rapidly, was in a peacetime frame of mind—the well-placed seek exemptions and the clever play the system, figuring out how to get around the rules. The Nixon controls, formalized in October 1971, were terminated in January 1973, the election of 1972 having been safely won. In June 1973 Nixon imposed some controls again; in 1974 Congress let his authority to impose controls lapse, except in regard to oil.[13]

That was a telling exception. All international oil trade is in dollars, and the Organization of Petroleum Exporting Countries (OPEC) responded to the closing of the gold window with a demand for higher prices. The oil-producing countries of the Middle East felt no pressure from Western military forces in the Persian Gulf; Britain withdrew its forces from the region at the end of 1971, and Nixon, preoccupied with Vietnam and facing congressional opposition to deployments in the region, declined to replace them.[14] OPEC took the occasion of the Israel-Egypt war of October 1973 to raise oil prices sharply—to the point that they had the same value as before August 1971 in terms of gold, but were far higher in dollars.[15]

Stagflation followed in the United States. In 1974 the gross domestic product fell .5 percent while inflation was 11 percent. In 1978, 1979, and 1980 the economy grew 4.8 percent, grew 2.5 percent, and fell .5 percent, respectively; inflation in those years was 7.5 percent, 11.3 percent, and 13.5 percent. This was not supposed to happen; the standard Keynesian doctrine said that higher unemployment reduced inflation and that higher inflation reduced unemployment. This failure of reality to conform to doctrine registered in the political process, and Federal Reserve chairman Paul Volcker's tight money and President Ronald Reagan's tax cuts produced low-inflation economic growth once again, for all but eighteen months of the eighteen years from 1983 to 2000.

But the existence of stagflation was not only a failure of macroeconomic doctrine; it was also evidence of the excessive Softness of the Big Unit private-sector economy. Big Business executives who felt themselves immune to the discipline of the marketplace eventually found out that they were not, and that profits could plunge and bankruptcy loom. Big Labor leaders who assumed that any wage and benefit increases could be passed along to consumers found out that they could not, and that their memberships could plunge and their bargaining power be reduced toward zero. Big Government officeholders who believed that the private-sector economy could be counted on to grow perpetually at any level of taxation and with any regime of controls found out that it could not, and that their job ratings could plunge and their careers be brought to an end at the polls. Softness turned out to be expensive. Excessive Softness turned out to be an expense the country could not afford.

Elite opinion in the years around 1980 was that the United States was in economic decline and that the decline could not be reversed. People just had to get used to living in an era of limits. This turned out to be a good prediction—for some countries in western Europe. Job growth in Germany, France, and Belgium—the core of the original European Union—has been minimal since 1980; economic growth has been tepid at best, far lower than in the United States; the increasing cost of generous welfare state benefits has required levels of taxation that are far above those in the United States but nevertheless are plainly inadequate to finance promised benefits for an aging population. But the prediction failed to come true in the United States. American economic success in the past quarter-century can be attributed in part to intelligent macroeconomic policy. It has come without a significant weakening of welfare state protections: Social Security benefits were made slightly less generous in 1983 and the Medicare program has undergone a number of adjustments, but only welfare payments to mothers of dependent children have been reduced appreciably.

There is another factor. Much of America's economic success has been the result of a Hardening of the private-sector economy. Unlike the extension of the Soft Social Security system, this was not the project of a small group of well-connected individuals, deftly taking advantage of political opportunities to advance their own long-term objectives. The Hardening of the private-sector economy has resulted mostly from actions not at the center but on the periphery, mostly in the private sector but on occasion in the government as well. With some exceptions, it has been the work not of university elites but of people seeking their own interests or advancing their own projects. In truth, these people have had little regard for whether they would

Harden the private-sector economy as a whole, but that Hardening has been the result. The process is not complete, and probably never will be.

Consider, for example, how the transportation industry has been significantly Hardened after decades of occupying a Soft niche. Ultimately what Hardened transportation in this country was government deregulation, but the impetus for this deregulation came from various individuals pursuing their own interests and goals over the years.

When the Depression of the 1930s put many truckers out of business, the New Deal tried to prevent a downward spiral by freezing things in place. Trucking companies were required to get certificates of convenience and necessity from the Interstate Commerce Commission (ICC) to transport any type of goods from any one point to another. If you got a certificate to transport horsefeathers from Pittsburgh to Cleveland, you had a monopoly over that trade unless and until someone else applied to the ICC for a certificate to transport horsefeathers from Pittsburgh to Cleveland—and you could intervene and oppose the application. Thus were created numerous Soft niches for trucking companies and for truckers, who were represented by the Teamsters Union. The Teamsters could negotiate generous contracts with the confidence that the costs could be passed along to consumers, thanks to friendly regulators. In the 1950s, the Teamsters Union started conducting nationwide bargaining sessions with the entire trucking industry, with the threat that if its demands were not met, all interstate trucking would be shut down.

In the 1950s, this cozy situation attracted the attention of a young Senate staffer named Robert Kennedy, the chief counsel of a Senate committee that was investigating connections between unions and organized crime. Kennedy became convinced that the Teamsters had many such connections and became obsessed, as chief counsel and later as U.S. attorney general, with the prosecution of Teamsters president James R. Hoffa. Kennedy, focusing on Hoffa's power to bring trucking to a halt nationwide, did not seem much concerned about the costs that the system of Soft trucking regulation was imposing on the country. But in the late 1960s, Ralph Nader, in *The Interstate Commerce Omission,* attacked that system for the way it stifled competition and raised prices for consumers. Nader's point, one on which free-market economists agreed, was that the government should not promote the cartelization of the economy.

In the late 1970s, Robert Kennedy's brother Senator Edward Kennedy took up Nader's point. Kennedy had already taken up the cause of airline deregulation. Since the New Deal, the Civil Aeronautics Board had had to approve all airline routes and fares; once again the idea was to freeze things in place, but in practice airlines sought (on occasion corruptly) political influence to get the routes and fares they wanted. (It was probably no accident that in the 1970s there was a convenient five P.M. flight from Washington Dulles Airport to Seattle, the home of Senator Warren Magnuson, chairman of the Senate Commerce Committee.) Kennedy and the Carter administration, usually at odds, cooperated in enacting airline deregulation, which enabled carriers to set routes and fares themselves (subject to airport capacity and safety standards). The result was intensive competition, new airlines, vastly reduced fares, and huge increases in the number of passengers. Perhaps because of his family's history with the Teamsters, Kennedy found deregulation of trucking a natural cause. The resulting law abolished certificates of convenience and necessity, and trucking firms could now seek customers and provide services where they chose. Railroad deregulation followed in the 1980s, and eventually the ICC was abolished.[16]

The deregulation of transportation made a Soft industry substantially Harder, and it squeezed enormous costs out of the American economy. Airlines had a hard time finding a successful business model but provided amazing service to passengers and shippers. Trucking firms burgeoned. Railroads modernized and prospered as they had not done for almost a century. Shipping of parts just-in-time for assembly in manufacturing, impossible under the old regulatory regimes, was now possible. These changes did not come without some cost. Airlines, trucking firms, and railroads facing Hard competition could not afford the kind of generous union contracts that regulated firms with Soft niches had granted. Old firms unable to profit in the new Hard environment went out of business. Unions lost members because most new firms were not unionized. But the number of people employed in transportation went up even as costs went down. And the safety record of the industries improved, contrary to the predictions of some critics of deregulation.

Transportation was not the only part of the economy

Hardened through deregulation—and, interestingly, it was not the only industry Hardened mainly because of efforts by the political left. Deregulating transportation was mostly the work of the Kennedys, Ralph Nader, and the Carter administration (though the Reagan administration also played a part), and in 1983 a liberal federal judge appointed by Jimmy Carter initiated the Hardening process of deregulating telecommunications when he ordered the breakup of the AT&T monopoly. As a result of Judge Harold Greene's decision, AT&T would have to spin off Western Electric, its research arm; the Bell phone companies would no longer have a monopoly on and maintain ownership of all the telephones in the country; and customers would have their choice of long-distance providers. (Some local areas were served by other telephone companies, but AT&T through its Bell affiliates had a near-monopoly.) Judge Greene was acting under the authority of the antitrust laws, and he reasoned that changing technology required changing the rules under which AT&T had operated for most of the twentieth century.[17]

Suddenly AT&T no longer occupied a huge Soft niche in the American economy. It would have to compete with phone instrument manufacturers and with long-distance providers (and, later, with mobile telephone companies), and it would no longer have a research affiliate it could finance with money acquired Softly through regulators. To be sure, telecommunications remains a highly regulated industry. (Hundreds of Washington-area private-school tuitions were paid for by fees to lawyers and lobbyists involved in passing the Telecommunications Act of 1996 and interpreting it in the years since.) But the economic savings to the country resulting from Judge Greene's decision have been enormous, and the Hard lash of competition has produced goods and services that the sluggish AT&T monopoly might never have put on the market. When I got two telephone lines at home in the early 1980s, I was told that there was no way the phone company could roll over calls from the first line, if it was busy, to the second unless the two numbers were consecutive. By the 1990s, the same phone company had figured out a way to do it. That may have required some great technological advance, but I doubt it; I suspect it was the spur of competition.

Other forms of deregulation have propelled the economy ahead. Deregulation of oil prices in 1982 resulted in sharp decreases in gasoline prices. Deregulation of natural gas in time produced plenteous supplies and low prices. Deregulation of electricity, a project of state governments more than the federal government, has reduced the cost to commercial users though not much to residential users. Some have argued that deregulation has had bad side effects. California suffered electricity blackouts in 2001 that many have blamed on power deregulation. But the problem was that, despite pleas from utilities, Governor Gray Davis in 2000 declined to release utilities from having to buy electricity daily on a spot market and to allow them to sign long-term contracts. When spot market prices spiked in 2001, the state was forced to buy electricity at the top of the market, and rates rose far more than they would have if Davis had heeded the utilities' plea the year before; this was one of the reasons Davis was recalled by the voters in

October 2003. The Northeast electricity blackout in August 2003 was also blamed on deregulation. But the problem was the transmission lines, one part of the system that had not been deregulated, leaving investors with no incentive to upgrade the electric grid.

But if government in some ways made the private-sector economy Harder, entrepreneurs did even more. This was not predicted: sociologist Daniel Bell wrote in 1963 that "in the modes of access to privilege, inheritance is no longer all-determining, nor does 'individual initiative' in building one's own business exist as a realistic route."[18] In 1975, as the nation was facing stagflation and Rabbit Angstrom was scampering from selling American cars to selling Toyotas, a nineteen-year-old Harvard dropout named Bill Gates and his friend Paul Allen wrote a software language for personal computers and founded a company named Micro-Soft in Albuquerque, New Mexico. Five years later the company, now called Microsoft and moved to Redmond, Washington, outside Seattle, developed the MS-DOS operating system and licensed it to IBM for its first personal computer. Shrewdly, Gates insisted that Microsoft retain rights to the software.[19] The computer industry had been organized vertically, with firms building their own hardware and developing their own proprietary software; the idea was to capture customers and hold them. Gates saw things differently. As business journalist John Heileman explains, "Side by side with Intel's Andy Grove, Gates envisioned a different structure, a horizontal structure, in which specialized competition would take place in each layer of the industry: chip company versus chip company, software company versus software company, computer company against computer company. He figured out, again with Grove, that the position of maximum power and profit in this new structure came from owning one of two critical industry standards: the OS [operating system] or the microprocessor. And, finally, he understood that Microsoft's control of the OS standard could be leveraged in ways that would give the company enormous advantages in competing for other software markets."[20]

Gates's insight was shrewd. IBM, the dominant computer firm in 1980, was wedded to the vertical structure and let Microsoft keep rights to the operating system. With its insistence on male employees wearing white shirts and ties, it was full of William H. Whyte's organization men and its bureaucratic procedures stifled innovation. Gates believed in small teams, originality, rapid decision-making, and informal clothes. By the early 1990s, IBM was in deep trouble and Microsoft had a higher market capitalization: Soft Goliath lost out to Hard David.[21] Yet even as he became the richest man in the world, Gates was still obsessed with competition. Unlike the General Motors executives of the early 1970s, he did not believe his company would be successful indefinitely. Someone else's innovation could do to him what competition had done to IBM. So in 1995, when Netscape announced its Internet browser, Gates ordered Microsoft to produce its own browser and abruptly switched the focus of the company to the Internet.[22] This triggered the government's antitrust case against Microsoft, but the company emerged without major damage, and Gates still claimed that he was running scared against possible competitors.

Gates was not unique. Other entrepreneurs with original ideas started small businesses which became giants and in the process made the private-sector economy Harder. Not all of them invented new products or services. In 1962 Sam Walton opened his first Wal-Mart store in Rogers, Arkansas. His idea was to create a chain of stores which would stock all manner of merchandise and sell it at consistently low prices. The going was slow at first. In 1970 the first distribution center was built in Bentonville, Arkansas, and in 1972 Wal-Mart was listed on the New York Stock Exchange. Wal-Mart developed key innovations, including a computerized inventory system that kept instant track of sales, along with distribution centers that kept stores stocked with items that were selling, which allowed Sam Walton's company to respond to signals sent in the Hard marketplace better than anyone else. Wal-Mart also emphasized hard-nosed negotiations with suppliers and a culture of friendliness toward customers. All of this worked: Wal-Mart became the nation's number one retailer in 1990 and expanded to Canada, Latin America, Germany, and South Korea. In 1997 it became the largest private employer in the world, with more than 1 million "associates." In 2002 its sales were $240 billion—$1.4 billion in a single day. Wal-Mart Hardened the entire retail sector of the economy; inefficient competitors went out of business or retrenched, and consumers got lower prices.[23]

In 1965 a senior at Yale named Fred Smith submitted a

paper for a management course proposing a new business. "The concept is interesting and well-formed," the professor wrote, "but in order to earn better than a C, the idea must be feasible." Smith's idea was a business which would provide one-day delivery of desperately needed items like computer parts and medical equipment anywhere in the United States. Smith did not get to act on his idea immediately; he served as a platoon leader and pilot in the Marine Corps in Vietnam. But in 1971, at the age of twenty-seven, he started Federal Express in his hometown of Memphis, Tennessee, financed by family money and venture capital investors. Packages would be picked up by trucks and delivered to airports all over the country, then flown to Memphis, sorted out and flown to their destinations, then delivered by truck in the morning. "When it absolutely, positively has to be there overnight" was one of Federal Express's sales pitches. FedEx, as it now is called, had imitators and competitors, but it has maintained its leadership position by adapting to the marketplace and motivating its employees by setting clear goals and rewarding extra effort—"getting discretionary effort out of people," as Smith has put it. "We still tell our employees what we always told them: You're delivering the most important commerce in the history of the world. You're delivering somebody's pacemaker, chemotherapy treatment for cancer drugs, the part that keeps the F-18s flying or the legal brief that decides the case." The defining concept of the company—absolutely, positively overnight—is inherently Hard.[24]

Another leader who built a great company was Jack Welch—with the interesting difference that the company he built, General Electric, was already one of America's largest and most profitable companies when he became CEO in 1981. Welch had an unusual career path. A railroad conductor's son from Salem, Massachusetts, he got a Ph.D. in metallurgical chemistry and joined GE in 1960, going to work at a small plastics operation in Pittsfield, Massachusetts. He helped develop an industrial plastic called Noryl, and in 1968—the year young Benjamin in the movie *The Graduate* was given one word of advice: "Plastics!"—Welch was made general manager of GE's $26 million plastics business. He rose rapidly as the units he headed logged big increases in revenues and profits. He spent most of his time on the road, visiting plants and customers across the country, and managed to convince higher executives to let him stay based in Pittsfield; only in 1977 did he move to GE's headquarters in Fairfield, Connecticut, where he was one of the competitors to succeed CEO Reginald Jones. Jones evidently admired the brash, competitive, innovative Welch, and he got the job at the age of forty-five. Welch believed that GE needed to "act fast and get the damn bureaucracy out of the way" and wanted every unit to "act like a small company": "I wanted GE to run more like the informal plastics business I came from—a company filled with self-confident entrepreneurs."[25] A large corporation had turned itself over to a small entrepreneur.

He made it a much larger corporation with a Hard entrepreneurial culture. Welch believed in differentiating between executives of different ability: "Differentiation is about being extreme, rewarding talent, and weeding out the ineffective." Managers had to separate those reporting to them into three groups: the top 20 percent, the vital 70 percent, and the bottom 10 percent. The top 20 got big bonuses and stock options, the vital 70 got some bonuses and stock options, and the bottom 10 were asked to leave General Electric. Welch decided that GE would remain only in businesses where it was the number one or number two; plodding along with low market share was demoralizing as well as unprofitable. So he sold off losing divisions and poured people and capital into businesses where the potential for profit was high, like GE Capital. At the same time he tried to create an "atmosphere of excellence where people dare to do new things" and insisted that "taking and missing a big swing is OK." Welch was surely the most admired executive of a large company in the 1980s and 1990s, a man who showed how even a large and diversified corporation could encourage the kind of entrepreneurial behavior which was changing and Hardening the private sector. During his twenty years as chairman, General Electric's revenues grew from $25 billion to $130 billion, and profits rose from $1.5 billion to $12.7 billion. GE met the Hard test of the marketplace: when Welch retired, it had the highest market capitalization of any company in the world.[26] GE accounted for a significant share of the increase in total market capitalization from $1.1 trillion in 1981 to $12.4 trillion in 2001. Moreover, the Hard example of General Electric inspired other large corporations.

Note that these entrepreneurs who did so much to change the private-sector economy and make it much more productive for the most part did not operate out of New York or Washington. Gates, Walton, and Smith built their companies far from those centers, in Redmond, Bentonville, and Memphis; Welch worked for years out of Pittsfield and was only at GE headquarters for four years before becoming CEO. Nor did they learn much of what made them successful from the nation's elite universities. Gates dropped out of Harvard, Walton graduated from the University of Missouri, Smith might never have started Federal Express if he had paid heed to his management professor at Yale, and Welch soon dropped the "Dr." he had earned as it became apparent that he was not just a research chemist.

Gates, Walton, and Smith all got the critical initial financing for their businesses from family money, which helped them obtain bank loans or venture capital; only after their companies operated successfully for several years did they go public. This was no accident: financing was hard to obtain for entrepreneurs in the 1960s and 1970s. The alternative minimum tax, enacted in 1969, raised the capital gains tax to a maximum of 49 percent, and interest income was taxed at a maximum rate of 70 percent—heavy disincentives to investors. In 1976 there were no high-tech startup companies founded, as compared to three hundred in 1968, before the alternative minimum tax was enacted.[27] Large corporations financed their capital investments with internally generated capital in the 1960s, but in the 1970s lower profits meant less internal capital to invest; meanwhile, the stock market remained in the doldrums, so capital was hard to raise there. And large corporations' research departments, as William H.

Whyte foresaw in the 1950s, produced little in the way of innovation.

The 1978 tax law lowered the maximum capital gains tax rate to 25 percent—a change which did much to invigorate financial markets in the 1980s. But invigorating them even more, at least in the long run, was another provision of the law which attracted little attention, Section 401(k). At the time most workers relied for retirement income on Social Security, personal savings, and defined benefit pensions from their employers—pensions which tied them to one employer for at least ten years and which obliged the employers to set aside huge funds for future payments, funds which were usually invested conservatively. In the years after passage of 401(k), many employers, to the surprise of experts, started switching from defined benefit plans to 401(k)s and other defined contribution pension plans, in which employers made one-time contributions to investment accounts controlled by individual employees. Internal Revenue Service regulations in the 1980s encouraged many employers to switch to defined contribution plans, and they were accepted by employees. These plans seemed more attractive after the highly visible failure of a few large defined benefit plans, including the LTV steel pension fund and the United Mine Workers' hospital fund. By 1998, the number of people covered by defined contribution plans had risen to 50 million, from 19 million in 1980; the number of people covered by defined benefit pensions had fallen to 23 million, from 30 million in 1980.[28]

The result was the infusion of vast sums into the financial markets in a way that helped change them to a force Hardening the private-sector economy. Individuals were now accountable for their own retirement funds, and in investing 401(k) money they could be less conservative and more venturesome than trustees of corporate pension funds. They could put their money into mutual funds whose managers' careers depended on achieving good rates of return. The growth of 401(k)s nurtured in increasing numbers of Americans an investor frame of mind, which appears to have motivated many more people to invest in the financial markets. Political pollsters noted that in 1992 only about 20 percent of voters were investors, while in 2002 about 60 percent were.

The financial markets were also Hardened by innovative financial entrepreneurs. One could cite many of them, but two of the most justifiably famous are Michael Milken and Henry Kravis. Milken grew up in Encino, in Los Angeles's San Fernando Valley, and graduated from UCLA and the Wharton School at the University of Pennsylvania. In 1978 he returned to Los Angeles and started working at the Century City office of the Drexel Burnham brokerage firm. Milken was one of several analysts who noticed something odd about the bond market. Most financial institutions and pension funds were required to invest in only investment-grade bonds, bonds rated BBB or higher. Non-investment-grade bonds were derided as "junk bonds." But Milken noted that the risk-adjusted returns for portfolios of junk bonds were quite high—they were not junk bonds but high-yield bonds. So Milken specialized in issuing and marketing non-investment-grade bonds. In so doing he channeled $26 billion to telecommunications and high-tech companies that could not have gotten financing otherwise—firms including MCI, McCaw, Viacom, TCI, Time Warner, Turner, Cablevision, News Corp., Hasbro, and Barnes & Noble. The use of high-yield bonds, business writer George Gilder writes, "frees capital from corporate bureaucracy and gets it into the hands of entrepreneurs." Gilder explains that in the 1980s General Motors invested $121 billion in research and development and capital investment while the market value of the company sunk to $22.9 billion; IBM invested $101 billion and its value dropped to $65 billion in 1990 and $41 billion in 1995. Milken and others, Gilder argues, "took the vast incarcerated capital resources trapped in old-line businesses and put it back into the markets."[29]

Milken was portrayed by much of the press as a predator, ousting incumbent executives and spurring firms to cut payrolls and phase out unprofitable activities. His career in corporate finance ended when he was convicted for insider training in relatively insignificant amounts. But high-yield bonds continued to be issued after his fall and made corporate America more efficient and profitable, generating new wealth that strengthened the American economy. In the 1950s and 1960s, large corporations had escaped Hard accountability in the financial markets because they generated enough internal capital to keep their businesses going in much the same fashion they had for years. In the 1980s and 1990s, thanks in large part to Milken, large corporations faced Hard accountability in the financial markets. And the American economy grew far faster than it had in the 1970s.

Henry Kravis, one of the partners in the investment firm Kohlberg Kravis Roberts (KKR), was one of many investment bankers playing a role in the Hardening of the American economy. Kravis grew up in Tulsa and went to Claremont College in California, then decided not to join his father's oil business. He went to work for Bear Stearns in New York, with his cousin George Roberts and Jerome Kohlberg, who pioneered the use of leveraged buyouts to enable owners of privately held family business to continue managing them. In 1976 the three formed their own firm, KKR, with $120,000 in capital. In 1979 they took their first publicly owned firm private in a leveraged buyout, by buying out the firm's stock. The investment firm could pay more than market price for a company's stock because interest on debt financing was tax deductible and could be deferred on high-yield bonds—which in the 1980s KKR got Milken and Drexel Burnham to market.[30] Leveraged buyouts became popular after former Treasury secretary William Simon in 1982 turned a $330,000 investment into $66 million, and KKR orchestrated some of the biggest—Beatrice Foods, Safeway, and others.

In 1987 KKR executed its greatest coup, the $25 billion leveraged buyout of RJR Nabisco. The story is told vividly in the 1990 bestseller *Barbarians at the Gate*.[31] The price of the buyout was raised by a bidding war between Kravis's associates and another group that intended to retain RJR Nabisco's CEO, Ross Johnson. Much of the journalism of the time cast buyout strategists as barbarians and incumbent executives as unfairly beleaguered philosophical leaders. But a fair reading of *Barbarians at the Gate* suggests that the barbarian is not Kravis but Johnson, who is shown sipping scotch when he should be concentrating on negotiations and who has the company maintain an eleven-jet corporate fleet with eighty-one people in the flight department. Kravis, in contrast, is shown as competitive but also civil and concentrating on business. And the RJR Nabisco buyout proved to be a success; the company managed to service its debt load. KKR now has a portfolio of fifteen companies with hundreds of thousands of employees and about $40 billion in revenue.

It is true that high-yield bonds were overused and leveraged buyouts much less common after the RJR Nabisco deal. As in commercial real-estate development or the venture capital–fed high-tech boom of the late 1990s, many of the first pioneers reaped huge profits and later operators paid too high a price for deals that went sour. But this is another way of saying that the Hard discipline of the market punishes excess in a way that is quickly apparent. *Entrepreneur,* a word hardly anyone used in 1980, was in common enough usage that George W. Bush included it, pronounced Texas style, in his standard stump speech in the 2000 campaign.

Though there are still Soft spots in the American private-sector economy, the Hardness that has been restored has led to economic growth and increases in productivity that almost everyone in the late 1970s despaired of ever achieving again. Certainly the extraordinary growth of the American economy in the 1980s and 1990s would have come as a surprise to Rabbit Angstrom. In his view the American Big Unit economy was doomed to decline, and by 2000 we would be feeding on table scraps. But Rabbit, like most elite experts of that era, did not anticipate the Hardening of the private-sector economy that produced such remarkable growth. This Hardening was the work of politicians and economists, of entrepreneurs and executives. Most were acting out of self-interest or in the pursuit of personal causes, but the combined result of their efforts was the resurgence of the American economy, which once again became, as it had been a century before, the prime engine of economic growth and prosperity in the world.

CHAPTER 4

HARDENING:

FROM *MR. SAMMLER'S PLANET*

TO THE 2003 BLACKOUT

In Saul Bellow's *Mr. Sammler's Planet,* published in 1970, Artur Sammler is a seventy-year-old Holocaust survivor living in his niece's apartment on West Ninetieth Street in New York City and spending his days at the New York Public Library. On his way home on the Riverside bus, he watches an elegantly dressed black man calmly pick pockets and pilfer purses. When Sammler gets off the bus, he goes to a pay phone to report the pickpocket to the police. "Of course the phone was smashed. Most outdoor telephones were smashed, crippled. They were urinals, also. New York was getting worse than Naples or Salonika. It was like an Asian town, an African town, from this standpoint."

When he finally does manage to reach the police, they are uninterested. Fascinated, Sammler continues to ride the bus each day and observe the pickpocket; then one day the pickpocket follows him, corners him in an elevator, and wordlessly exposes himself. Crime is all around: Sammler's niece's apartment is burglarized when she leaves a window unlocked.

Yet Angela Gruner, the rich daughter of the distantly related physician who got Sammler out of a displaced persons camp and brought him to New York, who after each of her visits to a psychiatrist on the West Side spends an hour with Sammler recounting the session, regularly "sent money to defense funds for black murderers and rapists." Angela is all for Softening America; Sammler sees the danger: "Listening to Angela carefully, Sammler perceived different developments. The labor of Puritanism was now ending. The dark satanic mills changing into light satanic mills. The reprobates converted into children of joy, the sexual ways of the seraglio and of the Congo bush adopted by the emancipated masses of New York, Amsterdam, London. Old Sammler with his screwy visions! He saw the increasing triumph of Enlightenment—Liberty, Fraternity, Equality, Adultery!" As for the growing criminal class, "the thing evidently, as Mr. Sammler was beginning to grasp, consisted in obtaining the privileges, and the free ways of barbarism, under the protection of civilized order, property rights, refined technological organization, and so on."[1]

Mr. Sammler's Planet was not one of Bellow's most favorably received novels; New York intellectuals who reflexively supported Softening policies in criminal justice, welfare, and education did not like to be reminded of the daily conditions of life in the big city that were the proximate result of those policies. Ordinary Americans were quicker to respond. Between 1970 and 1980 New York City's population fell by 1 million people—a middle-class exodus from which the city has never fully recovered. Other central cities also saw their populations plummet in these years, as their local police forces were unable to prevent huge increases in crime and as their generous welfare payments were creating a class of dependent mothers whose adolescent daughters would too often become dependent on welfare themselves and whose adolescent sons would too often grow up to become violent criminals.

Throughout the 1970s and 1980s and into the 1990s, the crime rate remained high—roughly on a plateau, with a lurch upward in the late 1980s and early 1990s generally ascribed to a crack cocaine epidemic. But the American public's response changed. While in the 1960s the prison population had fallen even as the crime rate increased, the prison population slowly increased in the 1970s, then around 1976 started to shoot upward. There were 196,000 prisoners in 1970, 240,000 in 1975, 315,000 in 1980, 480,000 in 1985, 739,000 in 1990, 1.085 million in 1995, and 1.321 million in 2000.[2] The prison population is affected not just by the number of people ordered to prison but by the length of their terms: sentence the same number of people to prison but double their sentences and in time you will come near to doubling the prison population. These numbers are mute evidence that a large decentralized mass of Americans—prosecutors, judges, jury members, and parole and probation officers—responded to high rates of crime by sending more offenders to prison and keeping them there longer. This was a quintessentially Hard response by a large cross section of ordinary Americans. If anything, the cross section was tilted toward political liberals, because elected officials and jury members in large central cities, where crime rates are highest, are more likely than Americans generally to be liberals.

It took much longer to reduce the number of crimes. Here the problem was the culture of police work. After the turmoil of the 1960s, big-city mayors, police leaders, and officials tended to be sensitive to, and often sympathetic with, the charge that police tactics in common use up through the middle 1960s amounted to police brutality. Policing methods therefore changed. Policemen (they were almost all men in those days) concentrated on responding to emergency calls—911 numbers and radio technology made this seem a sensible thing to concentrate on—and attempts were made to solve particularly violent and gruesome crimes. But, as Mr. Sammler found, the police had little interest in solving routine burglary and theft. " 'I understand,' " Mr. Sammler told the policeman who took his complaint about the pickpocket. " 'You don't have the personnel, and there are priorities, political pressures. But I could point out the man.' 'Some other time.' 'You don't want him pointed out?' 'Sure, but we have a waiting list.' 'I have to get on *your* list?' 'That's right, Abe.' 'Artur.' 'Arthur.' "[3] And policemen made no effort to police what criminologist George Kelling called "disorderly behavior," by which he meant "aggressive panhandling, street prostitution, drunkenness and public drinking, menacing behavior, harassment, obstruction of streets and public spaces, vandalism and graffiti, public urination and defecation, unlicensed vending and peddling, unsolicited window washing of cars ('squeegeeing') and other such acts."[4]

In 1982, Kelling and James Q. Wilson wrote an article for *The Atlantic Monthly* in which they argued that, among other things, the existence of broken windows in a neighborhood was a signal of disorder which told criminals and noncriminals alike that crimes would be tolerated and criminals would go unpunished.[5] Effective police action against disorderly behavior and disorderly conditions, they argued, would reduce the number of more serious crimes. But for many years police officials paid this advice no heed. The great vogue in the 1980s was community policing, which many police leaders described "in 'soft,' social science terms," said Kelling and Wilson. "In their view, community policing is antithetical to the 'crime-fighting' function that defined the role of police for decades." For cops on the beat, Kelling later wrote, it seemed "a strategy that is soft on crime, has little impact on it, emphasizes social work, cares more about the rights of the offenders than the interests of the community, and is in the 'grin and wave' tradition of community relations."[6] Such Soft policing predictably did not appreciably reduce crime. But police chiefs facing mayors and mayors facing voters argued that crime was just something people would have to endure, the product perhaps of an unjust society, an inevitable fact of modern urban life. Prison populations rose, but high crime rates continued.

In 1989 Kelling became a consultant to the New York Transit Authority police and helped design a program to end disorderly behavior in the subway. Turnstile jumpers were arrested, and it turned out that there were warrants out for the arrests of many of them on other, more serious charges. Those who lived in subways were forced out, and the Transit Authority successfully appealed a court decision declaring its actions illegal. Rudolph Giuliani, running for mayor in 1993, noted the success of the Transit Authority police and called for the arrests of squeegee men, who were shaking down motorists at streetlights and toll plazas, and of others guilty of disorderly behavior. Giuliani won, and he installed Transit Authority police chief William Bratton as his police commissioner, with Kelling as an adviser. From the top came orders: crime had to be reduced and disorderly behavior stopped—and precinct commanders who failed to achieve these goals would lose their jobs. Giuliani and Bratton ordered into place the CompStat ("computer statistics") system, which reported crimes instantaneously, allowing police to focus on high-crime areas and quickly track down criminals to prevent further crimes from occurring. And the Giuliani administration kept its word about making precinct commanders accountable: commanders were called in for monthly meetings, and those who failed to meet goals for crime reduction and did not have a good explanation left the meetings without their jobs. Commanders in a majority of the city's seventy-seven precincts were at one point or another fired. The word quickly got down. The *Daily News*'s Bronx police reporter told me that police officers on the beat in the Bronx were convinced that Giuliani knew how many crimes had been committed on their beat every day. Giuliani told me that he didn't quite know the statistics that well but that he had a pretty good idea at any time where crime-reduction goals were not being met. This was Hard leadership of the very highest quality. And the results were spectacular: within five years the number of major crimes was reduced by half and the number of murders by two-thirds. New York, long considered a crime capital, now had the lowest crime rates of any large American city—and lower crime rates than most of the major cities of Europe. The streets were suddenly safe and the city profited from an influx of tourists. Giuliani, a Republican in a heavily Democratic city, was reelected by a handsome margin. Seldom has a public policy so quickly and so spectacularly proved its worth.[7]

Others noticed. Giuliani's success was well publicized, and it led voters in other cities to ask their mayors why they couldn't reduce crime as Giuliani had. The political marketplace, Soft for a long time when voters saw little progress against crime anywhere, suddenly became Hard. Police officials from other cities went to New York to learn what their counterparts were doing and hired veterans of the New York experience to advise their departments. Crime declined across the nation, more in some places and less in others, but at record rates—by 32 percent between 1993, the year before Giuliani took office, and 2000, and by even more after that. It turned out that high crime rates were not inevitable. Hard penalties *and* Hard policing could make America a safer, less fearful, more pleasant country.

Interestingly, the elite institutions of the country did not produce this Hard solution. Criminology departments in the universities were and are dominated by advocates of Soft policies; George Kelling is a maverick in the profession. The *New York Times* excoriated Giuliani, at least until September 11, 2001, as a near-fascist whose policies were abusive to blacks and Hispanics—this despite the fact that the decline in the murder rate meant that *thousands* of blacks and Hispanics were alive who would have died had the rate remained what it was under Giuliani's predecessor. And the federal government had little to do with the reduction of crime. Congress tended to pass crime bills every two years, and President Bill Clinton made much of his provision purportedly paying for 100,000 more police officers. But in the work of reducing crime, Congress and Clinton were merely interested and occasionally helpful bystanders. The Hard work was done in the field, by Giuliani and Bratton and his successors, by a few intellectuals like Kelling and Wilson, and by the men and women of the New York Police Department and of other departments across the nation. Artur Sammler may or may not have lived to see the results, but Saul Bellow did.

It took just as long to Harden the welfare system. In 1965 Daniel Patrick Moynihan, then assistant secretary of labor, wrote *The Negro Family: The Case for National Action.*[8] Moynihan, a political scientist who made social science into an art, had noticed that nearly one-quarter of births to black women were, in the language then used, "illegitimate," and that while unemployment rates were declining, the number of welfare recipients was rising, "a startling increase in welfare dependency." Moynihan, as so often, identified a trend before anyone else, and long before it reached its apogee. His report was greeted with something like rage. He was "blaming the victim," critics said, trying to impose white middle-class values on blacks. The welfare rights movement and social work professors like Richard Cloward and Frances Fox Piven called for vastly increasing welfare benefits and piling up such costs that society would have to capitulate and provide a guaranteed annual income.

In the long run, most Americans came to see that Moynihan was right. When illegitimacy rates among blacks in central cities reached above 80 percent and welfare dependency peaked in the late 1980s and early 1990s—the same years when the crack epidemic resulted in record high rates of crime—the demand for change in the welfare system became overwhelming. But in the short run Moynihan's critics held sway over policy. Welfare spending rose from under $100 billion in 1970 to over $200 billion in 1980 and over $300 billion in 1990.[9] Political candidates, notably Ronald Reagan in 1980, fulminated against welfare spending. But officeholders did little about it.

The problem was the culture of the caregiving profession. For a moment in the late 1960s most voters and officeholders probably favored increased welfare spending. This was the moment when Americans were transfixed by the sudden discovery that poverty still existed in their midst and were persuaded by the argument that it was growing despite the increasing prosperity of the larger society. The social work profession and bureaucracy took shrewd political advantage of this and, fortified by court decisions, created a system that concentrated on providing the maximum amount of benefits for the maximum number of beneficiaries: evidently the view was that society must be made ever more Soft. The public bridled at the result but was unable to change the system. Federal bureaucrats unsympathetic to change maintained regulations that prevented states from changing rules; social workers on the ground unsympathetic to change made sure that the system kept on working as before. In the private sector, Softness could give way to Hardness because the discipline of profit and loss made the indefinite perpetuation of Softness after a time impossible. The public sector, in which programs' success is typically measured by the amount of inputs rather than the quantity and quality of outputs, resisted change much more successfully.

Moreover, the welfare system did not touch most Americans directly, as the criminal justice system did. Ordinary citizens have ways of influencing the criminal justice system directly—in electing prosecutors and judges, who tend to be judged primarily on their performance on criminal justice issues, and in serving on juries. Ordinary citizens do not have such direct means of affecting the welfare system. The officials responsible for its conduct are civil servants or department heads who are mostly immune to the judgments of the voters or elected officials who are judged on their performance on many issues.

Nevertheless, in time ordinary citizens did demand

changes in the welfare system, and some officeholders responded to the demand. Congress, prompted by Moynihan, in 1988 passed a law encouraging the states to experiment with work requirements for welfare. But most of the experimentation took place in state governments. Leading the way was Governor Tommy Thompson of Wisconsin, a small-town politician and veteran of state government first elected as governor in 1986. Wisconsin governors have extraordinary powers, notably a line-item veto that allows them to delete individual words and letters from laws passed by the legislature: you can do a lot if you are willing to line-item veto the word *not*. Thompson had the additional advantage of operating in a state capital, Madison, small enough that any knowledgeable veteran of state government knew the strengths and inclinations of state government professionals. Thompson used the flexibility provided by the 1988 federal welfare law and obtained waivers from Washington to restructure, step by step, the state's welfare program. Wisconsin offered jobs programs to welfare recipients and then imposed work requirements. The state provided aid—day-care allowances, transportation stipends, work clothes—to recipients who got jobs. The Thompson administration made clear that advancement in the welfare bureaucracy depended not on maximizing benefits but on maximizing jobs for welfare beneficiaries. Thompson extolled the benefits of the independence that a former welfare beneficiary gained from having a job, and in time that same attitude suffused the culture of the caregivers. Welfare officials across the state competed to take part in Thompson's latest programs.

When I visited Fond du Lac County, population 97,000, in 1997, the county welfare director boasted that the welfare rolls there had been reduced to zero. When Thompson left the governorship to become secretary of Health and Human Services in 2001, the welfare rolls in Wisconsin had been reduced by more than 90 percent.[10]

Other state and local officials had similar ideas. Governors John Engler of Michigan and Evan Bayh of Indiana achieved reductions in the rolls almost as great. In small states like Idaho, the welfare rolls almost disappeared. In New York, Mayor Rudolph Giuliani hired a veteran of Thompson's administration and cut the welfare rolls by more than 500,000. And this was not just a partisan Republican movement; Bayh was just one of the Democrats who achieved similar results.

It was against this background that the federal government passed the landmark 1996 welfare act. The welfare bill passed because of a political maneuver by the Republican Congress elected in 1994. Twice the Republicans passed bills changing the welfare and Medicare programs; twice President Bill Clinton vetoed them. The Republicans had planned to use these vetoes in what they expected would be a successful campaign against Clinton in 1996. But by July 1996 it was apparent that Republican nominee Bob Dole was not going to win. Speaker Newt Gingrich and other Republicans decided to pass the welfare portions of their previous bill, daring Clinton to veto them again. Clinton, after considerable delay and after receiving differing advice from his appointees, decided to sign the bill in August.

What followed was an astonishing nationwide reduction in welfare dependency. The welfare rolls peaked at 14.2 million in 1993, then began declining; in 1996, even before the passage of the federal law, the welfare rolls were down to 12.3 million, reflecting the success of changes in Wisconsin and other states. But the federal law had a profound effect: by 1999 the welfare rolls had been cut nearly in half, to 6.8 million; by 2001 the figure was down to 5.4 million.[11] At the same time, the number of children living in poverty was also going down. Unmarried mothers were evidently earning more in jobs or, in some cases, getting married and raising their incomes well above what they had been when they were on welfare. The percentage of black children living with two parents started to rise, for the first time since the 1960s. The recession of 2001 resulted in only slight increases in the welfare rolls and in children living in poverty in 2002.

One headline feature of the 1996 law surely played a major role: the provision limiting any welfare beneficiary to five years of benefits. This was Hard discipline, signaled even in the language used to redefine welfare programs: what for decades had been known as Aid to Families with Dependent Children (AFDC) became Temporary Assistance to Needy Families (TANF). In Fond du Lac County, I saw women walk out the door when the five-year limit was explained to them: better not to use up the benefits now, but to save them up for when they might really be needed, and go out and get a job. Previously, welfare recipients had been shown weeks-old lists of jobs and given little encouragement to apply. Now they were given up-to-the-minute computerized information about jobs and offered helpful hints on how to apply. Governors like Thompson and Engler got testimonials from former welfare beneficiaries on how much better their lives were now that they were economically independent and could stand up before their children as their provider. Undoubtedly some met hardships along the way. But the evidence is overwhelmingly in favor of the proposition that the 1990s change in the welfare system was one of the great public policy successes of recent times. A Soft zone of American life was made Hard, and people were better off.

It has proven more difficult to Harden the schools. The need was recognized two decades ago. "The educational foundations of our society are presently being eroded by a rising tide of mediocrity that threatens our very future as a nation and a people," read *A Nation at Risk,* the report of the National Commission on Excellence in Education in 1983. "If an unfriendly foreign power had attempted to impose on America the mediocre educational performance that exists today, we might have viewed it as an act of war."[12] Over the course of the twentieth century, education reports have been issued by various commissions, private and public, and some have had great influence over what goes on in classrooms. But *A Nation at Risk* got more attention from the news media and the public than all the others. One reason was what Diane Ravitch calls its "stirring language that the general public could understand."[13] But more important was the recognition that American schools simply weren't doing a good job educating children. SAT scores had plunged from their 1963 peak, the verbal SAT from 478 to the 420s in the late 1970s, the math from 502 to a low point of 466 in 1980.[14] Innovations that looked so promising in the late 1960s and 1970s—open education, alternative schools, the new math—had been abandoned; at their best they required a sensitivity and skill in teachers that was unrealistic to expect in a mass school system. Instead there was what Ravitch calls a "sustained assault on the academic curriculum in the late 1960s and early 1970s."[15] Academic requirements were abandoned and students allowed to take electives—filmmaking, mass media, driver education, consumer education, training for marriage and adulthood, values clarification. Foreign-language courses largely vanished. Absenteeism was increasingly tolerated. The amount of homework was sharply diminished. Grade inflation and social promotion became commonplace.[16]

What was the source of this Softness? One was the culture of the caregiving profession. The education schools since the 1920s had been teaching the virtues of Softness, constantly denouncing rote memorization and drill and arguing that children should learn on their own. And, as Diane Ravitch writes, "Since the 1930s, guidance professionals had maintained that students' mental health and personality adjustment depended on their sense of self-esteem. Many educators also held it as an article of faith that too much emphasis on academic achievement might impair students' self-esteem."[17] In addition, with rising enrollment of black and Hispanic students in the 1970s and 1980s, teachers lowered expectations and reduced requirements, as they had with the rising enrollment of the children of immigrants in the 1920s and 1930s.[18]

Teachers' unions also played a role in Softening the schools. In the late 1960s and early 1970s, teachers' unions effectively won the right to strike in most of the country. Albert Shanker, from the 1960s to the 1990s the head of the second largest teachers' union, the American Federation of Teachers, always insisted on the importance of high academic standards. But the National Education Association (NEA), by far the largest teachers' union, generally shared the education schools' hostility to Hard standards and enthusiasm for Soft schooling. Teachers' unions, like all unions, have an incentive to increase their members' pay and shield them from accountability—to make the profession Soft. It had long been difficult to transfer or fire a bad teacher—and teachers in every school building know who the bad teachers are—but with the success of the teachers' union movement, it became virtually impossible. In the late 1960s and early 1970s, the NEA vastly expanded its efforts into promoting strikes and political activism, led by officials from Michigan, who took the success of the United Auto Workers (UAW) in the 1930s and 1940s as their model. Like the UAW, the NEA saw itself as a force to protect workers from the rigors of Taylorite management, to increase pay and reduce accountability. But like the UAW, the NEA also accepted key elements of the Taylorite model—particularly the maxim that all employees are interchangeable and must be treated the same. This meant that management could not discriminate between workers, and therefore forbade merit pay and required teacher assignment strictly on the basis of seniority. As several scholars write, "Teacher union contracts in most cities also prevent schools from choosing teachers and assume that a good 'fit' does not matter: teachers are interchangeable and schools are created only by assembling standardized parts."[19] The immediate effect was that workers and teachers had more Soft protection.[20] But the ultimate effect for the public schools could prove to be the same as it was for the auto companies, which were not prepared to adapt to Hard competition when it emerged.

But it was not only the caregiving profession that promoted Softness in the schools. Parents, many busy with their own work in a Hardening private-sector economy, too often demanded little of the schools and in many cases protested angrily when their children were disciplined or received bad grades. So undemanding had high school become that parents encouraged their children to work after school or on weekends, to pay for brand-name clothing and expensive athletic shoes and make car payments, to the point that far more high-school students in the 1990s than in the 1950s were working after school,[21] even though Americans had become much more affluent in the intervening four decades. Nor was the desire to get into college a goad to achievement: fewer than a hundred of America's thousands of colleges and universities reject most applicants, and most high-school graduates are assured of admission to college or community college.[22] It is hardly surprising that a study of the high-school class of 2001 found that only 32 percent were qualified to attend a four-year college.[23] Just as Soviets used to describe their economic system by saying, "They pretend to pay us and we pretend to work," American high-school students could say, "They pretend to teach us and we pretend to learn." The course of least resistance, for teachers, parents, and students, was Softness.

A Nation at Risk changed attitudes. It was issued after a four-year period of low economic growth and high inflation and of huge layoffs in heavy-manufacturing industries like autos and steel. During the decade before its publication in 1983, the economy had changed. When my sister Marilyn Wagamon taught in Flint, Michigan, in the 1970s, she often urged students to go on to college. "Why should we do that?" they replied. "We can go out and get a job on the line at GM and right away make more money than you do" (teacher union contract terms were well publicized in Flint). Those who spurned her advice surely came to regret it: those jobs, so plentiful a decade before, had disappeared by 1983. It seemed increasingly obvious that to make a good living you had to have a good education: a Hard economy required Hard education. Polls showed that the public wanted higher standards, and states set up task forces and commissions to examine their schools' standards and curriculum.

But change came slowly or not at all. The culture of the education profession proved stronger and more resistant to change than the cultures of the criminal justice and welfare systems.[24] "A common observation among social service workers and foundation heads," write three social scientists, "is that big city public school systems are the toughest and least malleable bureaucracies they deal with."[25] Nostrums still flourished and grew. The cult of self-esteem continued strong throughout the 1980s, to the point that Education Secretary William Bennett noted that American students lagged behind students in other advanced countries in reading and math but ranked first in self-esteem. The "whole language" movement deemphasized phonics as a way of teaching English. California in 1987 adopted the whole language approach for the entire state, and test scores plummeted to the lowest in the nation; Superintendent of Public Instruction Bill Honig, later explained that he had made a terrible mistake in adopting the approach.[26] Another Soft program that held students back in California and other states with large numbers of Spanish-speaking students was bilingual education. Instituted in 1971 in response to a Supreme Court decision, bilingual education was supposed to be a way to enable Spanish-speaking students to keep up in math, science, and history while they learned English. But administrators and teachers, who got extra money for teaching bilingual classes, took to holding students in Spanish-language instruction (the Supreme Court decision concerned a Chinese child, but almost all bilingual programs are in Spanish) for three, five, or even seven years. The predictable result was that many students never mastered English sufficiently to qualify for higher education. Voters in California, Arizona, and Massachusetts in 1998 and 2000 passed laws requiring students to be transferred out of

Spanish-language instruction after one year, but bilingual education continues to retard the learning of English in many other states.

President George H. W. Bush's education summit in 1989, in which one of the most active participants was Governor Bill Clinton of Arkansas, called for the creation of national standards. But the national standards produced turned out to be useless. The National History Standards announced in 1994 included hundreds of teaching examples which the Council for Basic Education said presented "a disproportionately pessimistic and misrepresentative picture of the American past." The English standards were so insubstantial and jargon-ridden that Clinton's Education Department cut off their funding in 1994. The National Council of Teachers of Mathematics standards, introduced in 1989, deemphasized computation and, in Diane Ravitch's words, "consisted of nebulous goals that were admirable but difficult to implement, such as valuing mathematics, becoming confident problem solvers, reasoning and communicating mathematically and developing appreciation for the power of mathematics."[27]

But if the effort to impose Hard rigorous standards at the national level from the top down was mostly a failure, efforts to impose Hard standards at the state or local level from the bottom up may turn out to be more successful. These were partly prompted by the Clinton administration's 1994 education act, which included a Goals 2000 program to encourage states to set standards. They were also prompted by the spread of alternatives to the monopoly model of public schools. Free-market economist Milton Friedman long ago came up with the concept of school vouchers: instead of assigning children to public schools according to their place of residence, give their parents a voucher worth the amount of a year's schooling and let them choose which school—public or private—their children attend. In other words, replace monopoly with choice, bureaucracy with a market. Vouchers would subject the people who run public schools to Hard competition, and of course vouchers were and are opposed by public school administrators, teachers' unions, and (since teachers' unions have become one of the most powerful lobbying forces in just about every state capital) politicians.

But parents were not happy with their lack of choice and with the intractable education establishment. In the 1980s, Polly Williams, a black state legislator from Milwaukee and a supporter of Jesse Jackson for president, wanted to take her son out of one public school and put him in another. The school bureaucracy was unhelpful. Soon Williams was sponsoring a bill to provide school vouchers to Milwaukee parents, to be used at private schools, including religious schools. One of her key supporters was Michael Joyce, head of the Milwaukee-based Bradley Foundation, which funded research suggesting that vouchers could improve student performance and which provided scholarships for students at private schools. Another supporter was Governor Tommy Thompson, who got the legislature to vote for vouchers in Milwaukee in 1990. Not surprisingly, the Milwaukee school board opposed the program, initiating lawsuits to delay its implementation. But voters responded: they threw the pro-union members out and replaced them with pro–school choice candidates.[28]

The Milwaukee program became well known across the nation, and a similar school choice program began in Cleveland in 1995. In 1999 Florida passed a statewide program providing alternatives to children in failing schools.[29] Billionaires John Walton and Ted Forstmann set up a national program to provide private-school alternatives for children in failing public schools. Charter schools of varying types—public charter schools as well as schools set up by nonprofit organizations—were created in large numbers in a few states, in small numbers in many others. Private firms were being hired to run public schools in several central cities. Home schooling became much more common. For the first time, the people running the public schools faced competition, which threatened the flow of money into their systems.[30] They were being dragged, however slowly and despite their dogged resistance, toward Hard America.

So were students. Polls revealed strong support for high standards and accountability in the schools,[31] and in response state legislatures and governors adopted proficiency standards in reading, mathematics, and other subjects and set up testing systems to hold students accountable to those standards. The education act that George W. Bush called for in the 2000 campaign and that he signed in 2002, after some significant modifications by Congress, required states to establish standards and to make testing mandatory at certain intervals. Interestingly, the education bill received support from leading Democrats like Senator Edward Kennedy and Congressman George Miller, though it represented a sharp shift from the 1994 education act, which had rejected mandatory tests on the grounds that they would reflect adversely on schools in disadvantaged areas. But by 2001 and 2002, Kennedy and Miller agreed with Bush's argument that schools without Hard standards hurt poor and black children the most, since these students tended not to come from homes where learning was valued and reading encouraged. This was not the first time that those on the political left had advanced such arguments: in contemporary Britain the Labour Party's Tony Blair has made the same case, and in the 1930s the Italian Communist Antonio Gramsci countered the arguments of Fascist dictator Benito Mussolini, who had embraced the theories of American progressive educators.[32] They all recognized that Hard schooling promotes upward social mobility.

It is still unclear how Hard the standards and accountability will turn out to be. States have not yet reached the point where failure to meet Hard standards results in Hard consequences—being held back a grade or being denied a diploma. Already we see teachers and parents, alarmed by the large number who now fail to meet the standards, pressing to make the standards lower. Not many states tie specific standards to grade-to-grade curricula, which standards advocate E. D. Hirsch Jr. argues is necessary to spur achievement: "The few states, like Virginia and Massachusetts, that are farthest along that path, have made significant progress in both excellence and equity. The many states that lag behind in setting specific grade-by-grade standards have shown little educational progress."[33] One scholar grading the states' standards and accountability has found only five states with both solid standards and strong accountability[34]; fortunately, those five—Alabama, California, North Carolina, South Carolina, and Texas—include 25 percent of the nation's population.

So far we have not seen a substantial increase in student achievement. True, SAT scores for the high-school class of 2003 were the highest in thirty-five years, with a composite score of 1026, up from 1003 in 1992.[35] But fewer than half of high-school students take the SAT, and many of those who do have subjected themselves to the Hard competition of seeking places in selective colleges and universities. The National Assessment of Educational Progress (NAEP) tests in reading, mathematics, and science, administered to students in grades four, eight, and twelve—all nine-, thirteen- and seventeen-year-olds—have not shown much progress. The 2003 NAEP national tests showed little significant rise in reading scores since 1992, despite more than a decade of emphasis on basic reading skills. The 2003 math results were more encouraging, with some gains made since 1990, but the most recent NAEP science test, conducted in 2000, revealed no gain in American students' performance in science.[36] Education scholar Paul Peterson summarizes the long-term trends: "Some gains at the elementary level can be detected. Math scores have not slipped much since the 1970s—in fact they may have improved somewhat. But the overall effect is unmistakably grim. The United States has always trailed many other countries in math instruction, and there is no sign it has closed the gap. Verbal skills are even worse. Here there are multiple signs of a downward trend. Most disturbing, all signs of declining quality in test performance among high schoolers are accompanied by a decline in the percentage of students finishing high school. Students are walking away from public schools, choosing other ways of getting the apparent equivalent of a diploma [GED certificates]. They seem to understand, better than anyone else, that the American schoolhouse is badly in need of repair."[37]

Some evidence of progress has appeared in the results of some recent accountability tests, notably in Florida. While some critics of "high-stakes" tests ("high-stakes" because they affect promotion and graduation) have worried about whether such tests can accurately reflect student achievement, statistical comparisons with low-stakes test results suggest that the accountability tests are fairly constructed.[38] And there is considerable evidence that students in many voucher experiments where assignment of vouchers is by lot are doing better than those left behind in public schools.[39]

In the late 1980s and early 1990s, America's schools seemed hopelessly Soft, but in the intervening years, accountability and choice—Hardness—have become widely accepted as necessary to improve the schools. Public opinion polls reveal the solid support for accountability and choice, and many politicians—Democrats as well as Republicans—have endorsed Hardening the schools. The Hard offensive has made headway against the institutional interests of the teachers' unions and the caregiving culture of the education schools. As Terry Moe, a scathing critic of public schools and teachers' unions, writes, "For the most part, the unions have been successful at stalling or weakening these efforts [accountability and choice programs] to bring about real change in the system. But they haven't prevented them from gaining a foothold—and because each movement is backed by a movement with genuine power, there is every reason to believe that they will expand their turf in the years ahead."[40]

Hardening public-sector institutions is more difficult than Hardening private-sector institutions: a corporation cannot long ignore a failure to make profits, while a public-sector institution can ignore a failure to achieve results for a very long time indeed, as long as the revenue keeps flowing in. But public-sector institutions are also affected by the political marketplace. In criminal justice and welfare, public opinion for a long time sought Hardening and for years got very little. Then suddenly in the 1990s, crime and welfare dependency were cut in half. It is possible to hope that something like that will happen with education.

The last two decades of the twentieth century saw a Hardening of American criminal justice, welfare, and, to a very limited extent, education. The impulse for this Hardening came not from centralized elites, but from decentralized ordinary people, and it was resisted, to varying extents, by the professionals in each of these fields. That impulse found expression, sooner or later, in political candidates and public officials. It gained force because ordinary people could see in their daily lives the contrasts between the conditions produced by Soft criminal justice, welfare, and education and the conditions produced by Hard systems. Old people fearful of leaving their houses or apartments after dark because of crime could see how safe conditions were at suburban malls, which as private property were subject to Hard policing long before New York City was. Taxpayers seeing one generation of women after another living on welfare, in chaotic and criminal underclass communities, could also see immigrants coming to the United States from Latin America and Asia, raising families and working hard at jobs, and committing crimes and living on welfare far less often than underclass Americans. Employers dismayed by the high-school graduate job applicants who lacked basic reading and math skills also knew of the sometimes dazzling skills of slightly older Americans trained in colleges and universities, the people who helped produce the high-tech revolution that thrust America ever farther ahead of the rest of the world.

Ordinary Americans discovered that they didn't have to live on Mr. Sammler's planet, as the elite shapers and defenders of Soft criminal justice, welfare, and education policies insisted they did. And in time they were able to change those Soft policies and the culture of the caregiving professions. Just as the old corporate elites had resisted the Hardening of the private-sector economy, so did the old government and academic elites resist the Hardening of public-sector institutions. But the economic marketplace responded to Hard challenges, and, more slowly and haltingly, the public sector did as well.

The change can be seen on the streets of New York, in the electric power blackouts of 1977 and 2003. In 1977, Mr.

Sammler's time, there was rioting and looting in New York, as law-abiding citizens huddled in fear. In 2003, after the changes wrought by Rudolph Giuliani and the communal experience of September 11, 2001, there was no rioting or looting, and people congregated on the streets and restaurants handed out free food and bars free beer. A Harder America, it turns out, is a safer, friendlier, more helpful and self-disciplined society. The advocates of Softness wanted to make things easier on ordinary people, to save them from hardship, and to some extent they did. But excessive Softness, in the private or the public sector, turns out to create habits of the heart which make the economy less productive and creative and life nastier and more brutish. Mr. Sammler, who had seen things nastier and more brutish than anyone has ever seen in the United States, understood.

CHAPTER 5

HARDENING:
FROM *IF I DIE IN A COMBAT ZONE* TO THE IRAQ WAR

T he soldiers are hunkered down, under fire, at the beginning of Tim O'Brien's memoir of his service in Vietnam—less autobiography than literary imagination, he has said—*If I Die in a Combat Zone*, published in 1975: "We lay next to each other until the volley of fire stopped. We didn't bother to raise our rifles. We didn't know which way to shoot, and it was all over anyway. Barney picked up his helmet and took out a pencil and put a mark on it. 'See,' he said, grinning and showing me ten marks, 'that's ten times today. Count them—one, two, three, four, five, six, seven, eight, nine, *ten*! Ever been shot at ten times in one day?' 'Yesterday,' I said, 'and the day before that, and the day before that.' " The tone of weariness—and of futility—is unmistakable. " 'Captain says we're gonna search one more ville today,' Barney said, 'Maybe—' 'What's he expect to find?' Barney shrugged. He walked steadily and did not look back. 'Well, what *does* he expect to find? Charlie?' " Charlie was, of course, the name the soldiers used for the Viet Cong. " 'Who knows?' 'Get off it man. Charlie finds *us*. All day long he's been shooting us up. How's that going to change?' 'Search me,' Barney said. 'Maybe we'll surprise him this time.' 'Who?' 'Charlie. Maybe we'll surprise him this time.' 'You kidding me, Barney?' The kid giggled. 'Can't never tell. I'm tired, so maybe ol' Charlie is tired too. That's when we spring our little surprise.' 'Tired,' I murmured. 'Wear the yellow bastards down, right?' "[1]

Tim O'Brien, high-school class of 1964, was drafted in 1968, when Lyndon Johnson was still president, and in *If I Die in a Combat Zone* he accurately summarizes the strategy of Johnson and his military leaders: "Wear the yellow bastards down"—though they did not put it this way. Military historian Eliot Cohen writes that their strategy was based on a theory of "modulated application of violence." As for the Joint Chiefs of Staff, says Cohen, "one searches in vain for evidence that they had any strategic concept other than more intense bombing or the dispatch of more men to the fighting front. . . . The fundamental ground-war concept [was] attrition to grind the enemy into incapacity."[2] President Johnson and Defense Secretary Robert McNamara did little or nothing to elicit a better strategy from the Chiefs. Instead they relied on assurances from

General William Westmoreland, the Army commander in Vietnam from 1964 to 1968, that the war was going well, "a view resulting from a variety of quantitative indicators *all* of which would later turn out to be suspect." As McNamara indicates in one of his several memoirs, he focused "chiefly on the level of effort being made, not its fundamental direction."[3] This was Soft leadership, civilian leaders not holding military leaders accountable. Cohen writes contemptuously that Westmoreland "would not have lasted four and a half years in command under Lincoln. A Clemenceau would surely have visited him more than once or twice in his theater of war (and just for a few days). A Churchill would hardly have let him slip away without a constant, even brutal questioning of his strategic concept."[4] As another military expert puts it, "The Army ended up trying to fight the kind of conventional war it was trained, organized and prepared (and that it wanted) to fight instead of the counterinsurgency war it was sent to fight."[5] This translated into straightforward tactics: "a vast volume of firepower, the poisoning of large areas of vegetation, and a continuous effort to find the enemy and bring him to battle with American troops," writes Cohen.[6]

O'Brien shows what these tactics led to on the ground. The soldiers have reached the ville. "On the perimeter of the village, the company began returning fire, blindly, spraying the hedges with M-16 and M-70 and M-60 fire. No targets, nothing to aim at and kill. Aimlessly, just shooting to shoot. It had been going like this for weeks—snipers, quick little attacks, blind counter-fire. Days, days." The soldiers inspect the results—"the wreckage of huts and torn-down trees . . . debris, four smoldering holes in the dirt, a few fires that would burn themselves out." The military strategists depended heavily on quantitative indicators to gauge their success, but the men on the ground were not cooperating. "Captain Johansen told me to call the battalion headquarters. 'Just inform them that we're heading off for our night position. Don't mention this little firefight, okay? I don't want to waste time messing with gunships or artillery—what's the use?' "[7]

We are accustomed to thinking of war as an inherently Hard enterprise. People live or die, territory is won or lost, one side or the other is victorious. But it is not always so, and was not so for the United States in Vietnam. John Kennedy and Lyndon Johnson sent American troops to Vietnam not so much to win a victory as to prevent a defeat. Johnson feared that the Chinese Communists would flood Vietnam with troops as they had South Korea in November and December 1950; he also believed that the Soviet Union and China were allies, although information later available established that this was no longer the case. That is why Johnson insisted on approving all bombing targets in North Vietnam personally—a procedure for which he has been excoriated ever since. And it is also why Johnson did not proclaim, as Franklin Roosevelt had in 1941, that "the American people in their righteous might will win through to absolute victory." The United States never contemplated an effort to overturn the North Vietnamese government.

Whereas the American military in World War II knew that it had Hard work to do and set Hard goals for its men in arms, the American military in Vietnam let what had become its traditional ways of doing business undermine Hard goals. Soldiers were guaranteed a posting of no more than a year in Vietnam, and so men were constantly being shuffled into and out of the conflict. "Ticket-punching" officers were rotated in and out as well, looking at their service in Vietnam mainly as a useful way to further their military careers. These rotation policies fatally undercut unit cohesion—the trust and care for one another that soldiers develop from working together—which virtually all military experts agree is essential in war. Soldiers too often did not know their officers or their comrades. Military effectiveness was also damaged by Lyndon Johnson's refusal in 1965 to call up the reserves—in some cases, at least, older and more experienced soldiers than the young and not-very-well-trained draftees who were sent to Vietnam. So the United States had, in the words of military writer James Kitfield, "19-year-old draftees commanded by 22-year-old sergeants with shake-and-bake training."[8] College deferments were continued until 1968 and graduate school deferments until 1967, allowing many young men (including me) to avoid military service in a time of war. Why was that deferment policy continued for so long? Perhaps because the pool of military-age men was so large. The postwar baby boom produced a sharp increase in births in 1946, and those young men—the high-school class of 1964—turned eighteen just before Johnson vastly increased the number of American troops in Vietnam, in 1965.

Defense Secretary Robert McNamara tried to do in Vietnam what he had done as part of the stateside military in World War II: use statistics to measure military effectiveness. One such statistic was the infamous body count. McNamara believed that the Vietnamese Communists would quit fighting when they were losing more Viet Cong and North Vietnamese forces than they could replace, so officers were ordered to count the bodies of enemy dead to determine how many men they were losing. This attempt to create a Hard metric failed and instead laced Softness into the system. Was a dead Vietnamese in civilian clothes part of the enemy forces? Officers started to make up numbers to give their superiors the body count they wanted. Or, as Tim O'Brien indicates in *If I Die in a Combat Zone,* sometimes they would "waste time" reporting skirmishes to headquarters. This created a culture of dishonesty and corruption in the American military, and a deterioration of discipline. If officers were going to cheat, why shouldn't soldiers? Drug use became rampant, tensions between black and white soldiers often became violent, and even "fragging"—killing an unpopular officer—became common.

The military, especially the Army, was in bad shape after the last American forces left Vietnam in 1973. And, for the first time since 1948, there was no military draft. Richard Nixon, the target of angry student demonstrations on campuses and on the streets, correctly forecast that the demonstrations would mostly stop if the draft was abolished. Draft calls were reduced in 1969 and 1970, as Nixon's Vietnamization program required fewer soldiers. A commission appointed by Nixon recommended abolition of the draft in 1970. In 1971 the last draft notices went out. In 1972 Congress declined to reauthorize the draft and instead raised enlisted men's pay by 61 percent, a level 60 percent of that of a first lieutenant. The draft expired June 30, 1973.[9]

Most Army generals and military leaders opposed abolishing the draft, and many predicted that the Army could not be properly manned without it. In fact, the draft had created a Soft niche for the Army and, to a lesser extent, the other military services: they had not had to do much to compete for enlistments. The Army had filled most of its slots with draftees, and during the Vietnam War the other services had been assigned some draftees as well. The other services had had to compete for recruits, but recruiting efforts had consisted mainly of convincing young men subject to the draft that these other services were a more attractive option than the Army. With the draft abolished, however, the Army and the other services were in Hard competition for young men and women (Nixon's commission had recommended a much larger intake of women). Although the military could offer young men and women good pay, college bonuses starting in 1979, and G.I. Bill of Rights benefits (though the G.I. Bill was allowed to lapse in 1977 and was not revived until 1980), young Americans had many other career alternatives available to them. As James Kitfield writes, "The Army and the other military services were thus to be thrown into the open market in the bitter aftermath of Vietnam, vying for the services of one of the most antiauthoritarian and rebellious generations in modern American history."[10]

Not surprisingly, the quality of the all-volunteer force in the 1970s was notoriously low. The services had to accept large numbers of non–high-school graduates in order to meet their quotas—at a time when Soft education was making it very easy to graduate from high school. In the mid-1970s, most Marines had not graduated from high school. By the late 1970s, recruiting had become even more difficult: in 1979 the Army fell 11 percent short of its quota of 159,000 recruits—and at a time of economic turmoil, when the economic incentives for enlisting should have been more attractive. The problem seemed likely to get worse in the years just ahead. The sharp decline in the birth rate in 1962—the end of the postwar baby boom—meant that the number of young men and women of military age would start to decline precipitously in 1980. Conditions in the services were bad, and drug use remained a problem: on a confidential survey conducted in the late 1970s, 28 percent of service members said they had used illegal drugs in the previous month.[11]

But if the quality of many of the recruits was low, the quality of many of the officers who remained with the military in these difficult years was high. These men deeply resented the way their leaders had waged the Vietnam War, and they were deeply dismayed by many Americans' hostility to men in uniform. Instinctively they knew that war is a Hard taskmaster and that the American military had been Softened to the threshold of rottenness. The military needed to be reformed, to be Hardened, if it was to serve the American people as it should.[12]

The American military had deteriorated by the early 1970s in much the same way the large American industrial corporations had. They were organizations run on Taylorite principles: those in charge would prescribe what subordinates do to the lowest level of detail and would leave little to individual initiative. But Soft niches, protections for subordinates, and a failure to hold leaders and subordinates responsible for results created a culture of dishonesty, corruption, and insubordination. Soldiers did not care about the outcome of the war any more than auto assembly line workers cared about the quality of the cars rolling off the line.

In Vietnam, the standard American war doctrine—that the United States could win by attrition, by the steady and patient application of superior force—had not worked. Some American officers began worrying about whether the United States could win the next war—a war that could prove a far Harder challenge than Vietnam had been. In 1973, just months after the American command left Vietnam, General Donn Starry, head of the tank division at Fort Knox, visited Israel to be briefed on October's Yom Kippur War. The Israelis and their American tanks had been vastly outnumbered by the Egyptians and Syrians and their Soviet tanks; still, the Israelis had won. They had done it by outmaneuvering the enemy and using airpower to attack deep behind enemy lines. Starry knew that the Americans faced a potential crisis in Europe, for American tanks in West Germany's Fulda Gap were far outnumbered by the Soviet tanks just east of the Iron Curtain. He realized that the United States would have to employ similar tactics against a Soviet attack; otherwise the Soviets' firepower would overwhelm NATO forces before reinforcements could be sent in from overseas. Starry and General William DePuy, head of the new U.S. Army training and doctrine command (TRADOC), decided that the Army needed a new war-fighting doctrine. James Kitfield summarizes their conclusion: "The old industrial-mobilization model of warfare that the U.S. Army had long ago adopted was bankrupt. The Army would very likely have to fight and win the first battle of the next war."[13]

So began the development of the fighting tactics and training procedures that shaped the American victories in the Gulf War in 1991, in the Afghanistan campaign in 2001, and in the Iraq War in 2003. Progress came slowly. In 1976 General DePuy produced the new Active Defense war-fighting doctrine, but it was widely attacked as too traditional—just another attrition strategy. Then in 1982 General Starry and Lieutenant Colonel Huba Wass de Czege produced a new war-fighting document with the AirLand Battle strategy, emphasizing maneuverability, initiative, agility, depth of operations, and synchronization. In past wars the Army had performed badly in its initial engagements—the Kasserine Pass in World War II, Task Force Smith in Korea, the Ia Drang Valley in Vietnam. Now it had a war-fighting doctrine designed to produce "a unit ready to fight and win now." The new strategy led to new training procedures. Formerly the Army devoted a set amount of time to each step in training: Taylorite Softness. Now the Army required soldiers to pass tests showing they had mastered Step 1 before they were trained for Step 2: individual-oriented Hardness.[14] Hardness also effectively ended widespread drug use in the services, through a zero-tolerance policy pioneered by the U.S. Navy.[15]

A major influence in changing military tactics was Colonel John Boyd of the U.S. Air Force. Boyd was the best American fighter pilot in the late 1950s and much more than that: he developed the Energy-Maneuverability theory, which provided a quantifiable basis for developing aerial tactics; he was the single biggest influence in developing the F-15, F-16, and F-18; and in 1976 he developed what eventually became a six-hour briefing called "Patterns of Conflict."[16] In "Patterns of Conflict," Boyd emphasized the need for a rapid tempo in war-fighting, for disorienting the enemy, for bypassing hard resistance and making speedy advances, and for "fluid and fast-moving tactics that disrupted enemy thinking."[17] His mantra of "Observe, Orient, Decide, Act" became known as the OODA Loop and ultimately reached far beyond military circles. Though most Air Force and Army generals hated Boyd, his ideas were influential. Several officers who called themselves the Acolytes widely promoted Boyd's ideas, which by the early 1980s were at the center of the military reform movement. Boyd was in close touch with Wass de Czege when he was writing the AirLand Battle paper, and he frequently gave briefings at the Army's School for Advanced Military Studies, which Wass de Czege set up in 1983, and whose graduates became known as the Jedi Knights. Boyd's ideas were even more influential in the Marine Corps: the Marine commandant adopted Lieutenant Colonel Mike Wyly's doctrine manual that emphasized Boyd's central strategy—fluid, flexible fighting.[18]

The quality of recruits also improved sharply in the 1980s. In 1979 General Max Thurman became head of the

Army's Recruiting Command. He found that the Army was failing to meet its recruiting quotas and that some recruiting officers were cheating by helping unqualified teenagers enlist. Thurman put a stop to that and proceeded to lobby Congress to reinstate the G.I. Bill of Rights, with its education benefits, and to develop a new advertising campaign. Appeals to "duty, honor, country" were out; the new ads showed real Army soldiers—Thurman insisted there be no actors—and invited young people to "Be all you can be." Thurman succeeded in getting Congress to restore the G.I. Bill, and the ads' emphasis on training and benefits proved successful in attracting qualified recruits.[19] Cutbacks in force size after the 1991 Gulf War allowed standards to be made higher still,[20] and in 2002 Congress provided a program for college graduates to enlist for eighteen months in return for cancellation of college loans.[21] Since 1980, the services and the reserves have achieved their recruiting goals, except in 1998 and 1999,[22] and non–high-school graduates have become a rarity in the military. Racial conflicts, common in the 1970s, became uncommon in the 1980s, and the percentage of black officers and noncommissioned officers rose from 14 percent in 1970 to 31 percent in 1990.[23] Blacks now make up 12 percent of the officer corps; as a comparison, 8 percent of college-educated Americans are black. Hard rules—absolute commitment to nondiscrimination and uncompromising standards of performance—have made the military the part of America with the best relations between blacks and whites. It is a vivid contrast to colleges and universities, where blacks are admitted according to Softer standards than are applied to others, and where relations between blacks and whites are often tense.

In the Vietnam War the different military services rarely coordinated their actions; General Westmoreland pointedly refrained from obtaining a joint command, so orders for the Air Force and the Navy had to come from distant headquarters. The existing system, set up by the Defense Department authorizations of 1947, 1949, 1953, and 1958, made joint action next to impossible; not even Dwight Eisenhower could impose jointness. As a result, the services developed their own battle plans. The Joint Chiefs of Staff, trying to maintain service autonomy, declined to present a joint strategy; a decision by the Joint Chiefs required unanimous consent, and so their recommendations tended to be the lowest common denominator—a plan designed not to achieve victory but to minimize interservice disputes. The Joint Chiefs had found a Soft niche: knowing that civilian leaders had learned not to rely on their plans, they did not have to prepare joint battle plans for which they could be held accountable.[24]

But painful experience showed military leaders and members of Congress that this system did not work. One such experience was the failure of Desert One, the attempt to rescue the American hostages in Iran in April 1980. The operation involved only eight helicopters but still had to involve all of the services, and there was no joint organization capable of conducting it. As James Locher, an advocate of jointness, puts it, "The participating service units trained separately; they met for the first time in the desert in Iran, at Desert One. Even there, they did not establish command

and control procedures or clear lines of authority. Colonel James Kyle, who was the senior commander at Desert One, would recall that there were 'four commanders at the scene without visible identification, incompatible radios, and no agreed-upon plan, not even a designated location for the commander.' "[25]

Another painful experience was the 1982 bombing of the U.S. Marine barracks in Beirut, Lebanon, in which 241 Marines were killed. The official investigation afterward pinned much of the blame on confusing and dangerous rules of engagement that the unit's commander had been unable to get changed. And the reason the rules of engagement had not been changed was that the chain of command was so lengthy—extending from Beirut to the commander of the amphibious task force on ships offshore in the Mediterranean, to the commander of the Sixth Fleet in Gaeta, Italy, to the commander-in-chief of U.S. Naval Forces Europe in London, to the CINCEUR commander at SHAPE headquarters in Mons, Belgium, to the Pentagon and the secretary of defense.[26] Giving authority to a joint command directly accountable to the secretary of defense would have tightened that chain of command greatly.

Lack of jointness was even more apparent in the operation in Grenada that began just a day after the Beirut bombing. General Norman Schwarzkopf, aboard a Navy ship off Grenada, ordered the Marine colonel in charge of Navy helicopters to let Army men use them to rescue the American students at the nearby medical school; the Marine flatly refused (he was overridden by the admiral on board). And that rescue had been delayed for thirty-six hours because the medical school had been identified as a potential military target. Moreover, because Army officers did not know the communications channel to use in order to call in Navy fire support, Navy ships left Army Rangers unprotected on the beach. One Army officer found a phone booth and called North Carolina to try to coordinate Navy air support. The operation was ultimately successful, but eighteen Americans were killed and after-action reports pointed out many mistakes.[27]

These experiences made clear that military leaders and joint commanders needed a Hard system of accountability. The Navy resisted, as did most of the Joint Chiefs, who wanted to preserve the autonomy of their services. But one who advocated jointness and greater power for the chairman of the Joint Chiefs of Staff was the Joint Chiefs chairman himself, David Jones, who spoke out in 1982, a few months before his scheduled retirement. "There is reason to believe that, faced with a contingency requiring a major joint operation, our performance would be below the level we should expect or need," Jones said.[28] Then the political situation changed, making jointness possible at last. In 1985 Barry Goldwater became chairman of the Senate Armed Services Committee, and he wanted to make Pentagon reorganization the major achievement of his last two years in the Senate. Together with ranking Democrat Sam Nunn and Congressman Bill Nichols, a World War II veteran who had lost a leg in combat, Goldwater pushed through a bill to reorganize the Defense operational authority. The Goldwater-Nichols Act, passed in 1986, made the chairman of the Joint Chiefs the sole military adviser to the secretary of defense, freeing the chairman from having to overcome the vetoes of the service chiefs; created the position of deputy chairman; created a joint officer management system to remove the services' control over joint assignments; made the commanders of the regional joint commands directly responsible to the secretary of defense, not to the officers of each service; and required all combat forces to be assigned to the joint commands. No longer would military commanders have Soft niches protecting them from accountability; the streamlined chain of command would be flexible and responsive—prepared to meet the Hard challenges ahead.

The Hardening of the military's war-fighting tactics, its recruitment and personnel training, and its chain of command produced dramatic results. The first clear indication that this Hardening had worked was in the Gulf War of 1991. This was no war of attrition; it was a war of fast tempo, of lightning thrusts and disorienting the enemy. The land campaign was imaginative, with the Marines advancing deftly around obstacles along the coast to Kuwait and the Twenty-fourth Division of the Army going far out into the desert in a left hook to envelop Saddam Hussein's forces inside Iraq. The Marines also kept the Iraqis off balance by feigning an amphibious assault. The air war and the ground war were planned and executed separately and in sequence, but otherwise jointness characterized the operations. And the operations were remarkably smooth: only 147 American soldiers and sailors died in the Gulf War—a vivid contrast to the 47,414 who were killed in Vietnam and the 33,741 in Korea. John Boyd's admiring biographer

Richard Coram may have exaggerated, but only a little, when he wrote, "Everything successful about the Gulf war is a direct reflection of Boyd's 'Patterns of Conflict'—multiple thrusts and deception operations that created ambiguity and caused the enemy to surrender by the thousands. America (and the coalition forces) won without resorting to a prolonged ground war."[29] Indeed, General Norman Schwarzkopf's plans were drawn up by colonels from the School for Advanced Military Studies.[30] Boyd himself, before the House Armed Services Committee in April 1991, gave specific credit for the Gulf War victory to Huba Wass de Czege and Mike Wyly.[31] A Hard military produced a fast victory with low loss of life.

So it was also in Afghanistan in 2001. In the decade since the Gulf War, the Pentagon had produced a much greater number of precision weapons. Colonel Jack Warden, the architect of the Gulf War air campaign, has told how cumbersome procurement procedures made it difficult for the Pentagon to obtain compact GPS systems, so for the Afghanistan campaign officers went out to local electronics shops and bought compact civilian GPS gear and attached it to bombs. A Hardened military sought results and gave responsible individuals leeway to attain them. B-52s and B-1s, designed to deliver nuclear weapons to the Soviet Union, flew over Afghanistan and rained down relatively small precision bombs on targets identified by Special Forces officers or Northern Alliance troops riding horseback. Precision bombs were 10 percent of the munitions used in the Gulf War in 1991, 30 percent in Kosovo in 1999, and 70 percent in Afghanistan in 2001. The Taliban and Al

Qaeda were forced to flee or were captured or killed. Only seventy-four American troops died.

The military victory in Iraq in 2003 was even more spectacular. This was the first fully joint war. As military writer Fred Kaplan notes, "The institutional barriers of interservice rivalry, even hatred, were gradually broken down. Once new technologies made joint coordination possible, and once the war in Afghanistan showed that coordination could reap tremendous advantages, resistance seemed futile." The Army's Third Infantry Division made a deep thrust into the desert of Iraq, avoiding hard resistance and entering Baghdad in what was the most rapid infantry advance in history. Air Force, Army, Marine, and Navy units coordinated action in real time. Special Forces, highly trained and brilliantly led, were used more extensively than ever before, and to great effect—greater than is known at this writing, since much about their operations remains secret. (More will become known as reporters embedded with Special Forces, including my colleague at *U.S. News & World Report* Linda Robinson, write more about what they saw.[32]) Remarkably, only 140 American troops died during the main military action that ousted Saddam Hussein's regime from Iraq.[33]

The American troops who fought so successfully in Afghanistan and Iraq were, with their Hard goals and Hard training, a long way from the dispirited troops of the Soft Army in Vietnam that Tim O'Brien remembered. And a Hardening America has noticed the difference. Since the early 1990s, the military has been the institution most often rated as trustworthy by Americans. Examining the polls, two scholars note, "Baby boomers, with the effects of Vietnam still lingering, remain largely skeptical of the military. Yet the children of the baby boomers, with the effects of the first Gulf war coloring their view, are stronger supporters of the military than even their own Depression and World War II era grandparents ever were."[34] A Harder America seems on the horizon ahead.

THE BATTLE FOR THE
NATION'S FUTURE

Amanda Bright, the heroine of Danielle Crittenden's 2003 novel *amanda bright@home*, is a well-
educated thirty-five-year-old mother who has
chosen to leave her job and stay home to take care of her
small children: "Every time Amanda came home . . . she
felt asphyxiated by her small house. She stood for a
moment in the front hall, her arms full of grocery bags,
pushed from behind by two small children and thwarted
from moving forward by a minefield of rubber boots,
stuffed animals, and scattered blocks." Her husband, Bob,
works at the Department of Justice, and without her salary
from the National Endowment for the Arts (her job was
"writing press releases for events nobody ever attended")
they cannot afford a bigger house or any of the extras their

friends from school can. Visiting a friend at the country club swimming pool, Amanda looks at the stay-at-home mothers whose husbands have private-sector jobs: "They reminded her of prize thoroughbreds, retired from the track, content in their new vocation as broodmares. . . . Personal trainers kept their bodies buffed and sculpted purely for aesthetic pleasure, not because the women had any need to exert themselves physically." She listens as her friend Susie, in between stints as a daytime TV anchor, raves about her facial ("her skin had been sandblasted and troweled with Austrian mud"); later, standing in the toy-strewn chaos of her house, Amanda imagines Susie's Georgetown townhouse ("the sleek beige sofa with its row of silk cushions, unsullied by small fingerprints; the terry robe hung over the treadmill; that day's mail scattered over the polished wood floor").

But the knowing reader suspects that these luxuries may someday be Amanda's. The Justice Department has decided to go ahead with the antitrust case Bob has been working up against the software giant Megabyte. He tells her over dinner in the one nearby low-price restaurant they can stomach, "He seemed so alive and crackling with purpose that she felt . . . envious. . . . He was not just pulling ahead of his colleagues but soaring past her, and Amanda found herself unconsciously gripping the edge of the table, bracing herself against being buffeted by the force of his slipstream." Left unsaid is the likelihood that a good performance in the Megabyte case could put Bob in a position to make $500,000 a year, maybe $1 million, as an antitrust lawyer at a big firm.[1]

Amanda and Bob have made it, or are on the verge of making it, into a new American elite—what David Brooks (a contemporary and friend of Crittenden) calls the "educated elite." In *Bobos in Paradise*, Brooks describes how this new elite came out of "an America in which the bohemian and the bourgeois were all mixed up" ("Bobos" means bourgeois bohemians). But it is a Hard elite. "Previous establishments erected social institutions that would give their members security. In the first part of the twentieth century, once your family made it into the upper echelons of society, it was relatively easy to stay there," Brooks explains. "But members of today's educated class can never be secure about their own future. In the educated class even social life is a series of aptitude tests; we all must perpetually perform in accordance with the shifting standards of propriety, ever advancing signals of cultivation. . . . More important, members of the educated class can never be secure about their children's future. The kids have some domestic and educational advantages—all those tutors and developmental toys—but they still have to work their way through school and ace the SATs just to achieve the same social rank as their parents. Compared to past elites, little is guaranteed."[2] Amanda Bright and her husband certainly recognize the pressure: they feel lucky that, thanks to a family connection, their two young children have been admitted to a prestigious preschool—particularly because their son was nearly rejected for "poor scissor skills."

This is an elite that has been subject to Hard discipline—applying to selective colleges and universities and professional schools, wangling the best jobs in the public and private sectors, attracting the right mentors, producing high-quality work under deadline pressure. "The irony is that all this status insecurity only makes the educated class stronger," writes Brooks. "Its members and their children must constantly be alert, working and achieving."[3] But we know that Hard discipline produces good performance. The irony, then, is not that insecurity makes the elite stronger but that most members of the elite—certainly Amanda and Bob—favor public policies that increase the Softness in society. This was the impulse behind Hillary Rodham Clinton's health-care plan in the early 1990s and even behind the more modest programs that the Clinton administration pushed, like the family and medical leave law. Liberal elites have been the political allies of teachers' unions that have opposed Hardening the public schools— even if, like Amanda and Bob, they work to make sure that their own children get a Hard education.

The stubborn resistance to Hardening America's schools helps account for the fact that Americans up to age eighteen live mostly in Soft America, just as most Americans after the age of eighteen live in Hard America. This is the opposite of the situation in most of Europe, where high schools are Hard, to the point that students' performance usually determines how well they will do in the rest of their lives, and where life after high school is Soft, with generous welfare benefits, short work hours, long vacations, early retirement, and generous state pensions. American high school is so undemanding that 61 percent of high-school seniors work at jobs after school, on average for three hours a day—far higher than the 28 percent of high-school seniors in other advanced countries and astronomically higher than the 5 percent of American high-school students who worked after school in the 1950s. This is not because today's high-school students come from families with lower incomes than in the 1950s—parents today are much more affluent. Nor is it for the most part to save money for college: most of the students' earnings go to car payments, auto insurance, and clothing[4]—things young Americans today consider necessities, but which their parents are reluctant to pay for. Homework is often slighted, presumably because there is no Hard penalty for slighting it. Young Americans find a Harder environment on the job. In the 1980s, writer Ben Wildavsky found that 8 percent of all young Americans had worked at some time for McDonald's, and he pointed out that that experience taught them things high school didn't: "Most employees who pass through McDonald's gain the kinds of skills that help them get better jobs."[5]

After high school, Americans have many opportunities to obtain the Hard training that high schools mostly fail to provide. Nonselective colleges and universities have remedial courses to teach students what they should have learned in high school but didn't; in many schools more than half the students take such courses. In reporting for an article on immigrants, I found that many young Latinos master English and high-school math in community colleges; two of the nation's largest community college systems, in Los Angeles and Miami-Dade Counties, have student bodies (of 68,000 and 53,000, respectively) that are overwhelmingly Latino.[6] American colleges and universities are generally regarded as the best in the world, with Hard training in the sciences, mathematics, engineering, and economics; economics, the most rigorous of the social sciences, is also the only one that has moved politically to the right in the past three decades. Professors enjoy the Soft security of tenure but are usually inspired to produce original work by competition and peer pressure and because they are motivated people who chose academic careers over others that probably would have been more lucrative. The humanities and, to a lesser extent, the social sciences have been Softened since the 1960s, taken over by tenured radicals who fight tenaciously to exclude all others from their ranks. Still, there is some Hardness left, and the professional schools remain Hard. The Armed Forces provide plenty of Hard training for thousands of young men and women. Vocational schools and apprenticeships provide Hard training for trades and crafts in which young people can make good livings doing work they like; these seem to attract primarily young men, who may end up making better livings than do many of the young women who now make up a large majority on college campuses. For adults seeking a college degree and a course of study relevant to their work, there is the University of Phoenix, an accredited, for-profit institution with campuses in business-friendly locations all over the country. This is a booming business; John Sperling, the university's founder, owns stock worth hundreds of millions of dollars.

All of these post-secondary institutions have Harder standards than most high schools. Many drop out of these Harder institutions, and there are consequences for doing so in a country with a Hardened private sector in which you need skills to make good money. As Wildavsky notes, "A surprising number of burger flippers advance through the ranks and enjoy the benefits that go with managerial responsibility in a demanding [Hard] business. . . . Far from sticking its workers in an inescapable rut, McDonald's functions as a de facto job training program by teaching the basics of how to work."[7] This was one of the lessons of the welfare work requirements of the 1990s: the best job training is a job. And one job can lead to another. In mid-century America, with its Big Units, young people expected to get a job with one corporation and stay with it until retirement.[8] A high-school graduate in Flint could get a job on the line at GM and stay there until he retired, with handsome benefits, at fifty-five. In twenty-first-century America, with its burgeoning small businesses, young people expect to move from one job to another several times. When they leave one job, they have the Soft protection of unemployment benefits and credit cards to tide them over and the confidence that in a Hardened economy other opportunities will appear. They also have the option of self-employment or working as a temp—both fast-rising parts of the American economy.[9]

And Americans are happy in their work. Intellectuals imagine that most Americans are unhappy with their work: novelists write of the deadening toil of boring jobs and academics talk about alienation and anomie. But that is only a reflection of how intellectuals think they would feel if they had to do the kind of work that they imagine most of us are doing. Americans might be unhappy if their work was the Taylorite plodding for big corporations that mid-century experts predicted for us. Amanda's husband, Bob, loves his work, and so do most Americans even though they don't have the responsibility of running the case against Megabyte. In recent polls the percentage of Americans saying they were not satisfied or only a little satisfied with their work reached record lows. Two-thirds would take the same job again. Only two in ten are dissatisfied with their job security. In fact, most put a priority on the rewards available in Hard America rather than the security that Soft America could offer: two-thirds would prefer a higher-paying job they could lose to a low-paying job they could be sure of keeping. Very large majorities say their employers are accommodating in letting them take care of family needs. Two-thirds would continue to work even if they had enough money to live comfortably the rest of their lives. Three-quarters are satisfied with the amount of leisure time they get.[10] Moreover, as the *Wall Street Journal* noted, polls show that "most of us also feel our own loyalty to our own companies is reciprocated, and that our employers care for us."[11] All this at a time when more adults are working longer hours than they did a generation ago.

One gets the sense from these poll results that America's rapidly changing economy has been generating choices that enable very large majorities of adults to find satisfying work. The number of deadening jobs has surely declined as technology has advanced. Even assembly line work now leaves the worker freer to do the job his own way, as Taylorite management has largely been abandoned and workers or teams of workers are expected to show initiative in achieving goals and are held responsible for the results. The educated elite assumes that ordinary people who are not managing the Megabyte case are dissatisfied with their work. But that is condescending and wrong. Most Americans understand that people have different skills and ambitions, priorities and interests. Some want to spend more time with family and friends or on community activities than others. Those who do can seek Soft niches with tenure; there still are such niches and always will be. Others seek various kinds of work with Hard standards, and evidently they mostly find it. They get a sense of accomplishment from their work, from achieving Hard goals and measuring up to Hard accountability. They get a sense of honor, whether their accomplishments are recognized by the whole nation, by others with whom they work, by their families and friends and neighbors, or just by themselves. Achievement of Hard goals can be rewarded by money, as it usually is in the private sector; by promotion, as it usually is in the public sector; or simply by self-recognition. For we gain happiness not only from pleasure but also from the performance of duty, and from the honor it provides. Hard America is a happy America.

At the opening of the twentieth century, American life seemed too Hard, and the nation used some of the prosperity that was the product of a Hard economy to make life Softer. At midcentury, it seemed that everything was fated to get even Softer, and many things did. The Big Unit private sector was laced with Softness, the country (spurred by the success of the civil rights movement) was turning toward Softness in criminal justice and welfare dependency, and the Hardening of education in response to *Sputnik* turned out to be only temporary. But by the beginning of the twenty-first century, large parts of America had become much Harder—the private-sector economy, criminal justice, welfare, the military. There were even gathering signs of a Hardening of the schools.

Twentieth-century Softening was largely the product of elites—the advocates of the regulatory state and welfare state protections, the progressive educators, professors in the schools of social work and criminology. Twentieth-century Hardening has been the project not of university and media elites but of decentralized individuals. Some have aimed specifically at Hardness in the public sector—Rudolph Giuliani and Tommy Thompson and John Boyd. Their successes had a demonstration effect: once they were recognized, the demand in the political marketplace for others to follow their example became impossible to resist. The Hardening of the private sector has been the work of entrepreneurs and executives who were not necessarily interested in Hardening but were pursuing original visions of how to get rich—Sam Walton, Bill Gates, Jack Welch, Michael Milken, Henry Kravis, and many others. They saw opportunities that others missed and they—and others—could measure their success by the Hard metric of profits and stock prices. The result was rapid wealth creation and "creative destruction"—Joseph Schumpeter's term for the way market capitalism wreaks change that creates many more opportunities for others.

The general trend in America since the 1960s has been toward Hardening. The private sector has been vastly

Hardened, and prosperity and the ability to make our livings doing interesting and congenial work are the results. In the public sector, welfare and criminal justice have been Hardened after the disastrous Softening of the late 1960s and early 1970s. The Softness encouraged by racial quotas and preferences seems likely to persist for at least another generation. But many black Americans have chosen to escape the Soft niches that racial quotas and preferences create for them and to make their way in Hard competition: the black CEOs of Time Warner, American Express, and Merrill Lynch are only the most visible of the millions of black Americans who have taken advantage of the opportunities Hard America offers. The military has been Hardened for all the world to see, in the amazing, ultra-low-casualty victories in the Gulf in 1991, Afghanistan in 2001, and Iraq in 2003.

Talent pushed us toward Softness. Genius pushed us toward Hardness. John Dewey and the first progressive educators, the apparat of men and women who put together and extended the Social Security program, were people of talent who persistently and effectively Softened the Hard America of Theodore Dreiser. Sam Walton and Bill Gates, John Boyd and Rudolph Giuliani, were people of a certain genius who persistently and effectively Hardened the Soft America of the late 1960s and early 1970s, against determined opposition. But others have contributed to America's Hardening, more quietly and even less noticed— unknown engineers and teachers and craftsmen and civil servants and corporate executives have also sent out ripples of Hardness, strengthening the muscle tone of the nation.

Will the Hardening of America continue? Or will we move toward a Softer America as the twenty-first century goes on? Battles over Hardening and Softening go on all the time. At the margins there is almost always room for argument. Are a particular state's welfare work requirements too stringent, or not stringent enough? Are a particular state's high-school English and math standards too demanding? It is not difficult to imagine reasonable arguments on both sides. We know that competition and accountability—Hardness—tend to bring out the best in people. But we also know that sometimes competition and accountability can be too harsh. Early-twenty-first-century America has many Hard standards that are appropriate for different kinds of people. Take Special Olympics, the splendid organization set up by Eunice Kennedy Shriver which sponsors athletic contests for people with mental retardation. To some, Special Olympics may sound Soft: every competitor who shows up and completes the race gets a prize. But actually this is Hard competition. Special Olympians must do something that is difficult for them; they must appear before hundreds of people and complete a particular athletic course. This Hard competition elicits effort and performance that people used to think the mentally retarded were incapable of. The obvious joy of many Special Olympians at their achievement shows that they know they have achieved respect and honor.

Many social critics look back on the past with nostalgia. But in the turn-of-the-century Hard America of *Sister Carrie,* many Americans faced a difficult, even cruel existence. The Softened America of the second half of the twentieth century created terrible problems of its own. Indeed, from the vantage point of the early twenty-first century, the Softened Americas of *Rabbit Is Rich, Mr. Sammler's Planet,* and *If I Die in a Combat Zone* look like dystopias. The Hardened America of the present is a much better place. And the future can be better still.

Many future battles over Hardening and Softening will, of course, take place in the political arena. President George W. Bush has been a consistent advocate of Hardness. He is a member of the high-school graduating class of 1964 and graduated from Yale and Harvard Business School, but he does not share the liberal baby boomer elite's conviction that ordinary people who did not achieve similar success in Hard schools are in need of Soft protection. Bush, as some distressed conservatives have noticed, has not sought a smaller government (domestic discretionary spending in his first three years rose more than in Bill Clinton's last three) or a more decentralized government (his education act gives the federal government a greater role in setting educational standards than ever before). What is consistent about Bush's major programs is that they have promoted competition and accountability: Hardness. This is what ties together his educational standards, his support of individual investment accounts in Social Security (which would give individuals more control and therefore responsibility over retirement savings and government less), his lower tax rates (which increase incentives to earn in the marketplace), his prosecution of the war against global terrorists. It may seem odd that Bush, whose success in the private sector was at best mixed, should promote competition and accountability; perhaps it is because he has gained satisfaction from his greater success in the Hard competition of electoral politics and public-sector governance.

Bush's Democratic opponents, meanwhile, have *not* been consistent advocates of Softness. After all, a significant number of Democrats worked to Harden criminal justice and the welfare system in the 1990s; Bill Clinton bragged that his temporary subsidies for police positions helped reduce crime, and, after some hesitation, he did sign the 1996 welfare act. As in the past, however, Democrats (and some Republicans) have sought to Soften economic life for Americans through incremental measures—HMO regulation, prescription drug benefits, universal preschool. They seldom if ever address the argument that moving in this direction would eventually produce a Soft welfare state like those of western Europe, with high pensions and early retirement, with little flexibility and therefore low growth and high unemployment. When pressed, they argue that America is so far from a European system that the danger isn't worth worrying about.

But Hardening and Softening occur over time, and we need to be alert to the fact that decisions made today could have profound consequences for our future. As this is written, we are heading into another presidential campaign, one in which important questions of Softness and Hardness are at stake. Two key issues will be whether to retain the Bush tax cuts and whether to add individual investment accounts to Social Security. Lower tax rates create Hard incentives to earn and leave less room for new Softening federal programs. Individual investment accounts would move Social Security in the same direction the private sector moved private pensions by switching from defined benefit plans to defined contribution plans: more Hard responsibility on the individual, less Soft dependence on Big Unit corporations and unions. The decisions voters make in 2004 could do much to determine how Soft and how Hard this nation is in 2014, 2024, and 2034.

On the issues of welfare dependency and criminal justice, the battles are being fought on the margins. On welfare, liberals want to reduce work requirements and to provide more exceptions to the five-year limit on welfare payments. But even if such changes are made, the Hardness of the system is likely to endure. Knowing that benefits are temporary and that work will at some point be required has changed the attitudes and actions of millions of Americans. In criminal justice, serious arguments are being made that the five-year minimum sentences for possession of illegal drugs are too Hard—that they are unjust and that they are causing more criminal behavior than they prevent. And various states have seen movements to legalize marijuana for medicinal purposes: referenda to permit this have passed in some states, and campaigns for those propositions have been financed, interestingly, by billionaire arbitrageur George Soros and University of Phoenix founder John Sperling.

The military after its impressive victories in Afghanistan and Iraq still must deal with the demands of what William Lind and others have called "fourth generation warfare."[12] The military, against great internal resistance, has mastered what Lind calls "third generation warfare"—maneuver rather than attrition, with fast tempo, disorientation of the enemy, lightning thrusts. Fourth generation warfare consists of attacks by unconventional forces—terrorists, guerrilla organizations, or terrorist groups that to a considerable extent are criminal gangs, like the IRA in Northern Ireland and the FARC in Colombia. "Fourth generation warfare seems likely to be widely dispersed and largely undefined," writes Lind. "The distinction between war and peace will be blurred to the vanishing point. It will be non-linear, possibly to the point of having no definable battlefields or fronts. The distinction between 'civilian' and 'military' may disappear. Actions will occur concurrently throughout all participants' depth, including their society as a cultural, not just a physical, entity. . . . Success will depend heavily on effectiveness in joint operations as lines between responsibility and mission become very blurred."[13] In Iraq, facing attacks from Baathists and Islamist terrorists, the military has gained great experience in dealing with such organizations and the unorthodox tactics they use. But it will be hard work to refashion the Hard military to fight a considerably different type of battle from what it has known even in the recent past.[14]

The schools remain one part of American society that is largely, though not entirely, Soft. Polls make it clear that the public wants greater accountability in education, and through the political marketplace that desire has forced the passage of accountability laws in the states and by the federal government in 2002. But the breakthrough experienced on welfare and crime has clearly not occurred yet.

The Softening impulse is still strong in the culture of the caregiving profession and maybe never will abate. Already we have seen efforts—successful in some places, unsuccessful in others—to Soften accountability standards and to Soften the consequences for failing to meet those standards. Voters may tell pollsters that they want tougher standards, but parents, by not demanding more of their children's schools and by acquiescing in their teenagers' desire to work after school at the risk of not completing homework, have indicated that Hard standards may not be so important to them.

But perhaps they are important to their children. Teenagers working after school may be seeking, and in any case are often getting, the Hard standards they don't encounter during school hours. In the book *Millennials Rising,* published in 2000, William Strauss and Neal Howe argue that the teenagers of the 1990s were very different from the Generation X teenagers of the 1980s: more focused on achieving goals, more interested in serving others, more eager to meet Hard standards than to take it easy under Soft standards. Strauss and Howe portray them as self-starters, eager to be of service to others, quick to form community organizations: "They will rebel against the culture by cleaning it up, rebel against political cynicism by touting trust, rebel against individualism by stressing teamwork, rebel against adult pessimism by being upbeat, and rebel against social ennui by actually going out and getting a few things done."[15] Robert Putnam in *Bowling Alone* noted similar encouraging signs about young Americans in the late 1990s.[16] The Hard success visible in the adult world all around these young Americans may be making them dissatisfied with the Softness of their schools and seeking Hardness—before eighteen in group projects and after-school jobs, and after eighteen in college and the military and the private sector. If European students in Hard schools mostly yearn for Softness, American students in Soft schools seem increasingly to be yearning for and reaching out to Hardness.

Strauss and Howe argue that their Millennial generation, those born between 1982 and the present, have been raised more carefully and monitored more closely than the generation of Americans before them. Certain changes in family patterns in recent years go some way toward supporting their argument. There have been small declines in the rate of divorce. There have been increases in the percentage of children living with two parents—notably, the first increase in the percentage of black children living with two parents since Daniel Patrick Moynihan identified a downward trend in 1965; this may have been spurred by changes in the welfare laws. And there has been an increase in the percentage of mothers of small children remaining at home rather than taking jobs.[17] By 2003, 10.5 million children had stay-at-home moms, up 13 percent over the previous decade; there were also 189,000 children with stay-at-home dads.[18] Amanda Bright is not alone. All these changes add up to more parental involvement with their children—and just about all the social science shows that children do better when there is more parental involvement. These changes may also reflect an increasing awareness that raising children is a Hard task, in which you are held accountable for results, and that delegating that task to others—when a father leaves his wife and children or when parents put their children in day care or with baby-sitters—is not without its costs.

September 11 taught us that there are things we cannot delegate to others. United Flight 93 was the last of the four hijacked planes to take off, because of delays at the Newark airport. That meant that the passengers had time—109 minutes—after the hijackers launched their attack to respond. Prior to September 11, the standard injunction to passengers and crew on a hijacked airliner was to cooperate and not resist, the assumption being that the hijackers want to land the plane somewhere and that the only way to survive is to acquiesce. But passengers on United Flight 93 called their loved ones on cell phones and heard the terrible news of the attacks on the World Trade Center and the Pentagon. It quickly became obvious that these hijackers had no intention of landing the plane safely. So the passengers got together and resisted. "Let's roll!" were the last words Lisa Beamer heard husband Todd Beamer say. We do not know exactly what happened: the tapes that have been released to relatives of the dead passengers and crew members are reportedly terrifying. But we do know that United 93 came down in an empty field in Shanksville, Pennsylvania, far short of the hijackers' intended destination—probably the U.S. Capitol. As columnist Brad Todd wrote five days later, "Just 109 minutes after a new form of terrorism—the most deadly yet invented—came into use, it was rendered, if not obsolete, at least decidedly less effective. Deconstructed, unengineered, thwarted, and put into the dust bin of history. By Americans. In 109 minutes."[19]

An alert citizenry, as law professor Glenn Reynolds writes on instapundit.com, is "a pack, not a herd." Not a herd of sheep waiting to take direction from a single dog, but a pack of wolves, each alert and ready to act together with others to defend themselves against deadly attack. The attackers of September 11 and other Islamist terrorists are eager to destroy America and Americans in any way they can: as Hard a threat as our country has ever faced. Americans since September 11 have shown themselves to be a pack, not a herd, ready to defend ourselves and our civilization—whether the attack comes on us as members of a military unit or as members of the general public going about our lives the way we usually do. September 11 has made us understand even better that Soft America lives off Hard America, that while we act reasonably in keeping parts of American life Soft, we depend for our prosperity and our advancement and our existence on the parts of America that are Hard. The boundary between Hard America and Soft America is ever shifting, going this way and that in different parts of American life. But we should never forget that we need to maintain a solid core of Hardness, to remind ourselves that only in facing competition and accountability can we be sure to have the strength we need to survive and prevail against our deadly enemies. And that we will be rewarded with honor as we do.

NOTES

CHAPTER 1

1. Theodore Dreiser, *Sister Carrie* (New York: Bantam, 1982), 1–8.
2. Diane Ravitch, *The Troubled Crusade* (New York: Basic Books, 1983), 45.
3. Richard Sennett, *Families Against the City* (Cambridge: Harvard University Press, 1984), 107–8.
4. www.infoplease.com/ipa/A0760610.html.
5. Robert Kanigel, *The One Best Way* (New York: Viking, 1997), 19.
6. Ron Chernow, *Titan* (New York: Random House, 1998), 478.
7. Eric Goldman, *Rendezvous with Destiny* (New York: Vintage, 1955), 86–88, 90–92, 113–14.
8. On Wisconsin and other states, see Eric Goldman, *Rendezvous with Destiny*, 132.
9. John Milton Cooper, *Pivotal Decades* (New York: Norton, 1990), 214–15.
10. Robert Wiebe, *The Search for Order: 1877–1920* (New York: Hill and Wang, 1967), 145.
11. For Dewey on education, see Alan Ryan, *John Dewey* (New York: Norton, 1990), 133–42; Diane Ravitch, *The Troubled Crusade* (New York: Basic Books, 1983), 45–48.

12. Robert Wiebe, *The Search for Order: 1877–1920*, 152, 151, 149.

13. Alan Ryan, *John Dewey*, 139.

14. John Dewey, *My Pedagogic Creed*, in *Early Works*, v. 5, p. 86, quoted in Alan Ryan, *John Dewey*, 135.

15. Diane Ravitch, *The Troubled Crusade*, 58–59, 79.

16. Diane Ravitch, *The Troubled Crusade*, 43.

17. Diane Ravitch, *The Troubled Crusade*, 55.

18. Education Policies Commission, *Education for All American Youth*, 142, quoted in Diane Ravitch, *The Troubled Crusade*, 62–63.

19. Diane Ravitch, *The Troubled Crusade*, 45.

20. Diane Ravitch, *The Troubled Crusade*, 55.

21. Diane Ravitch, *The Troubled Crusade*, 55–56.

22. See Robert Kanigel, *The One Best Way*.

23. Daniel Patrick Moynihan, *The Politics of a Guaranteed Income* (New York: Random House, 1973), 20.

24. Derek Leebaert, *The Fifty-Year Wound* (Boston: Little, Brown, 2002), 223–26.

25. Eric Larrabee, *Commander in Chief* (New York: Simon & Schuster, 1987), 6.

26. Derek Leebaert, *The Fifty-Year Wound*, 226.

27. Derek Leebaert, *The Fifty-Year Wound*, 224.

28. William H. Whyte, *The Organization Man* (New York: Simon & Schuster, 1956). Contrary to usual practice, I have used his middle initial, because there was another well-known writer at that time (cited in *The Organization Man*) named William Foote Whyte.

29. William H. Whyte, *The Organization Man*, 255.

30. William H. Whyte, *The Organization Man,* 76, 78ff, 129, 137, 205–17, 243–48.

31. Sloan Wilson, *The Man in the Gray Flannel Suit* (New York: Four Walls Eight Windows, 2002), 36; William H. Whyte, *The Organization Man,* 132.

32. Robert D. Putnam, *Bowling Alone* (New York: Simon & Schuster, 2001).

33. Diane Ravitch, *The Troubled Crusade,* 69–79.

34. Seymour Martin Lipset and William Schneider, *The Confidence Gap* (New York: Free Press, 1983).

CHAPTER 2

1. Raymond Chandler, *The Long Goodbye* (New York: Ballantine, 1971), 1.

2. *The Raymond Chandler Mystery Map of Los Angeles* (Los Angeles: Aaron Blake Publishers, 1985); Edward Thorpe, *Chandlertown* (New York: St. Martin's Press, 1983), 153.

3. Michael Barone, *Our Country* (New York: Free Press, 1990), 200.

4. Jane Jacobs, *The Economy of Cities* (New York: Random House, 1970), 151–54.

5. Michael Barone, *Our Country,* 163–64.

6. Michael Barone, *Our Country,* 75, 164.

7. Derek Leebaert, *The Fifty-Year Wound,* 213.

8. Diane Ravitch, *The Troubled Crusade,* 76.

9. Diane Ravitch, *The Troubled Crusade,* 228–33.

10. Barbara Olson, *Hell to Pay* (Washington, D.C.: Regnery, 1999), 39–45.

11. Rich Lowry, *Legacy* (Washington, D.C.: Regnery, 2003), 11.
12. Nancy Altman, forthcoming biography of Cohen, Ball, and Myers.
13. Walter McDougall, *The Heavens and the Earth* (New York: Basic Books, 1985), 243.
14. Walter McDougall, *The Heavens and the Earth*, 307–24; Charles Murray and Catherine Cox, *Apollo: The Race to the Moon* (New York: Simon & Schuster, 1989), 77–79.
15. Walter McDougall, *The Heavens and the Earth*, 361–77.
16. Charles Murray and Catherine Cox, *Apollo: The Race to the Moon*.
17. Homer Hickam, "NASA's Vietnam," *Wall Street Journal*, August 29, 2003.
18. Gregg Easterbrook, "Beam Me Out of This Deep Trap, Scotty," *Washington Monthly*, April 1980.
19. Rand Simberg, "Past Perfect, Future Misleading," Foxnews.com, August 28, 2003.
20. See www.xprize.org.
21. Walter McDougall, *The Heavens and the Earth*, 413.
22. See John Dollard, *Caste and Class in a Southern Town* (Madison: University of Wisconsin Press, 1988).
23. Michael Barone, *Our Country*, 19; Gavin Wright, *Old South, New South* (New York: Basic Books, 1986).
24. Stephan Thernstrom and Abigail Thernstrom, *America in Black and White* (New York: Simon & Schuster, 1997), 132–36; Michael Barone, *Our Country*, 353–58.
25. See the poll results in Stephan Thernstrom and Abigail Thernstrom, *America in Black and White*, 139–41.

26. Stephan and Abigail Thernstrom, *America in Black and White*, 158–61.

27. *Historical Statistics of the United States* (Washington, D.C.: U.S. Department of Commerce, 1975), 413.

28. *Historical Statistics of the United States*, 420.

29. Stephan Thernstrom and Abigail Thernstrom, *America in Black and White*, 263–65.

30. Michael Barone, *Our Country*, 371.

31. Charles Murray, *Losing Ground* (New York: Basic Books, 1984), 56–68.

32. Michael Barone, *Our Country*, 371–73.

33. Charles Murray, *Losing Ground*, 154–66.

34. Charles Murray, *Losing Ground*, 9.

35. Stephan Thernstrom and Abigail Thernstrom, *America in Black and White*, 428.

36. Stephan Thernstrom and Abigail Thernstrom, *America in Black and White*, 386–422.

37. John McWhorter, quoted in Damon Linker, "Victimology," *Commentary*, October 2000, 77–78; John McWhorter, *Losing the Race* (New York: Free Press, 2000), 123–24.

38. Greg Winter, "New Ammunition for Backers of Do-or-Die Exams," *New York Times*, April 23, 2003.

39. Diane Ravitch, *The Troubled Crusade*, 233–34.

40. Diane Ravitch, *The Troubled Crusade*, 234–66.

41. Diane Ravitch, *The Troubled Crusade*, 326.

42. Charles Reich, *The Greening of America* (New York: Bantam, 1971), 6–9.

43. Charles Reich, *The Greening of America*, 17.

44. Charles Reich, *The Greening of America*, 16, 18.

45. Charles Reich, *The Greening of America*, 18, 427.

46. Charles Reich, *The Greening of America*, 19.

CHAPTER 3

1. John Updike, *Rabbit Is Rich* (New York: Ballantine, 1981), 7, 11, 13, 12.

2. John Kenneth Galbraith, *The New Industrial State* (New York: Signet, 1967), 13–26.

3. John Micklethwait and Adrian Wooldridge, *The Company* (New York: Modern Library, 2003), 117, 116.

4. David Halberstam, *The Reckoning* (New York: Morrow, 1986), 24.

5. William Serrin, *The Company and the Union* (New York: Random House, 1974), 310–11.

6. David Halberstam, *The Reckoning*, 23.

7. David Halberstam, *The Reckoning*, 55.

8. John Micklethwait and Adrian Wooldridge, *The Company*, 129.

9. John Micklethwait and Adrian Wooldridge, *The Company*, 129–30.

10. John Micklethwait and Adrian Wooldridge, *The Company*, 125, 129.

11. Robert Skidelsky, *John Maynard Keynes: Fighting for Freedom, 1937–1946* (New York: Viking Penguin, 2000).

12. Robert Bartley, *The Seven Fat Years* (New York: Free Press, 1992), 27–28, 36.

13. Robert Bartley, *The Seven Fat Years*, 29–31.

14. Henry Kissinger, *Years of Upheaval* (Boston: Little, Brown, 1982), 669. This decision, which amounted to

NOTES

saying that the United States had a greater interest in a country that produces rice than in countries that produce oil, gets one paragraph of discussion in this 1,214-page memoir.

15. Robert Bartley, *The Seven Fat Years*, 32.
16. Robert Kennedy, *The Enemy Within* (New York: Harper, 1960); Evan Thomas, *Robert Kennedy* (New York: Simon & Schuster, 2000), 74–89, 273; Adam Clymer, *Edward Kennedy* (New York: Morrow, 1999), 227–30, 234–37, 242; Robert Fellmeth, *The Interstate Commerce Omission* (New York: Viking, 1970).
17. Steve Coll, *The Deal of the Century* (New York: Touchstone, 1988).
18. Daniel Bell, *The Radical Right* (New York: Ayer, 1977), 17.
19. Ken Auletta, *World War 3.0* (New York: Broadway Books, 2001), ix; John Heileman, *Pride Before the Fall* (New York: HarperCollins, 2001), 56–61.
20. John Heileman, *Pride Before the Fall*, 57.
21. John Heileman, *Pride Before the Fall*, 59–63.
22. John Heileman, *Pride Before the Fall*, 63–66.
23. Wal-Mart Stores, Inc. History, Walmart.com; "Business: Wal-Mart Takes It All," www.activewomensclub.dk/Stoppress/030306_walmart_takes_it_all.asp.
24. Charles Fishman, "Face Time with Fred Smith," *Fast Company*, June 2001, 64; Fred Smith, "How We Got Started," *Fortune*, www.fortune.com/fortune/fsb/specials/innovators/smith.html; "Federal Express," *Wikipedia*, www.wikipedia.org/wiki/Federal_Express.
25. Jack Welch, *Jack* (New York: Warner, 2001), 44, 56, 92.

26. Jack Welch, *Jack*, 25, 159, 449, 450, 31–32, 362.
27. Robert Bartley, *The Seven Fat Years*, 67.
28. Michael Barone, "Changes for the Better," *U.S. News & World Report*, April 28, 2003, 32.
29. George Gilder, "Mike Milken and the Two-Trillion-Dollar Opportunity," *Forbes ASAP*, April 10, 1995.
30. Academy of Achievement, Henry Kravis interview, www.achievement.org/autodoc/page/kra0int-4, www.achievement.org/autodoc/page/kra0int-2; Thayer Watkins, KKR, www.sjsu.edu/faculty/watkins/kkr.htm.
31. Bryan Burrough and John Helyar, *Barbarians at the Gate* (New York: HarperCollins, 1990).

CHAPTER 4

1. Saul Bellow, *Mr. Sammler's Planet* (New York: Viking, 1996), 7, 12–14, 45–50, 17, 31, 32, 7.
2. *Statistical Abstract of the United States 1998*, 229; *Statistical Abstract of the United States 2002*, 202.
3. Saul Bellow, *Mr. Sammler's Planet*, 13–14.
4. George Kelling and Catherine Coles, *Fixing Broken Windows* (New York: Touchstone, 1998), 15.
5. James Q. Wilson and George Kelling, "The Police and Neighborhood Safety," *The Atlantic Monthly*, March 1982, 29–38.
6. George Kelling and Catherine Coles, *Fixing Broken Windows*, 145.
7. Much of this is based on my own reporting during

the period, as well as on numerous journalistic accounts.

8. Daniel Patrick Moynihan, *The Negro Family: The Case for National Action* (Washington, D.C.: Office of Planning and Research, United States Department of Labor, March 1965).

9. Michael Tanner, *The Poverty of Welfare* (Washington, D.C.: Cato Institute, 2003), 36.

10. This account draws on my own reporting, particularly in Wisconsin and New York City.

11. *Statistical Abstract of the United States 2002,* 353.

12. National Commission on Excellence in Education, *A Nation at Risk* (1983), 5.

13. Diane Ravitch, *Left Back* (New York: Simon & Schuster, 2000), 411.

14. Diane Ravitch, *Left Back,* 410.

15. Diane Ravitch, *Left Back,* 408.

16. Diane Ravitch, *Left Back,* 403–07.

17. Diane Ravitch, *Left Back,* 426–27.

18. Diane Ravitch, *Left Back,* 404.

19. Paul Hill et al., "Minority Children at Risk," in Paul Peterson, ed., *Our Schools and Our Future* (Stanford: Hoover Institution Press, 2003), 131.

20. Terry Moe, "The Politics of the Status Quo," in Paul Peterson, ed., *Our Schools and Our Future,* 206.

21. *Third International Math and Science Study,* 1998, National Center for Education Statistics, cited in Jo Thomas, "Experts Take a Second Look at Virtue of Student Jobs," *New York Times,* May 13, 1998.

22. Albert Shanker, "A Landmark Revisited," May 9, 1993, reprinted in *Education Next*, Spring 2003.
23. Manhattan Institute, "Public High School Graduation and College Readiness Rates," September 17, 2003.
24. Paul Peterson, ed., *Our Schools and Our Future*, 8–10.
25. Paul Hill et al., "Minority Children at Risk," in Paul Peterson, ed., *Our Schools and Our Future*, 130.
26. Diane Ravitch, *Left Back*, 443–48; interview with Bill Honig.
27. Diane Ravitch, *Left Back*, 431–41.
28. Dan McGroarty and Bob Smith, *Trinnietta Gets a Chance* (Washington, D.C.: Heritage Foundation, 2001).
29. Terry Moe, "The Politics of the Status Quo," in Paul Peterson, ed., *Our Schools and Our Future*, 198–99.
30. Paul Peterson, ed., *Our Schools and Our Future*, 8.
31. Public Agenda, *Where We Are Now: 12 Things You Need to Know About Public Opinion and Public Schools* (2003), 8–9.
32. E. D. Hirsch Jr., *The Schools We Need* (New York: Doubleday, 1996), 6.
33. E. D. Hirsch, "Neglecting the Early Grades," in Paul Peterson, ed., *Our Schools and Our Future*, 299.
34. Herbert Walberg, "Real Accountability," in Paul Peterson, ed., *Our Schools and Our Future*, 319.
35. Greg Toppo, "SAT Takers Are Sharpening Up," *USA Today*, August 27, 2003.
36. nces.ed.gov/nationsreportcard.
37. Paul Peterson, "Little Gain in School Achievement," in Paul Peterson, ed., *Our Schools and Our Future*, 68–69.
38. Jay Greene et al., "Testing High Stakes Tests," Man-

hattan Institute Civic Report, February 2003, www.-manhattan-institute.org/html/cr_33.htm.

39. Terry Moe, "Real Choice," in Paul Peterson, ed., *Our Schools and Our Future*, 340–41.

40. Terry Moe, "The Politics of the Status Quo," in Paul Peterson, ed., *Our Schools and Our Future*, 205.

CHAPTER 5

1. Tim O'Brien, *If I Die in a Combat Zone* (New York: Broadway Books, 1999), 2, 4.

2. Eliot Cohen, *Supreme Command* (New York: Simon & Schuster, 2002), 177–78, 179.

3. Eliot Cohen, *Supreme Command*, 181, 182–83.

4. Eliot Cohen, *Supreme Command*, 183.

5. Andrew Krepinevich, *The Army and Vietnam* (New York: Olympic Press, 1986), 271.

6. Eliot Cohen, *Supreme Command*, 181.

7. Tim O'Brien, *If I Die in a Combat Zone*, 7, 8.

8. James Kitfield, *Prodigal Soldiers* (New York: Simon & Schuster, 1995), 367.

9. Michael Meese, "The Army Officer Corps in the All-Volunteer Force," *Contemporary Economic Policy*, April 2002, 101.

10. James Kitfield, *Prodigal Soldiers*, 134.

11. David King and Zachary Karabell, "The Generation of Trust," *American Enterprise*, July 2003.

12. On these officers, see Colin Powell, *My American Journey* (New York: Random House, 1995); Rick Atkinson, *The*

Long Gray Line (New York: Simon & Schuster, 1999); James Kitfield, *Prodigal Soldiers.*

13. James Kitfield, *Prodigal Soldiers,* 151–55 (quotations on pages 154, 155); Richard Lock-Pullan, " 'An Inward Looking Time': The United States Army, 1973–76," *Journal of Military History,* April 2003.

14. Richard Lock-Pullan, " 'An Inward Looking Time': The United States Army, 1973–76"; Romie L. Brownlee and William J. Mullen III, *Changing an Army* (Carlisle, Penn.: U.S. Military History Institute, 1985), 68–101. 202.

15. James Kitfield, *Prodigal Soldiers,* 229–30.

16. Robert Coram, *Boyd* (Boston: Little, Brown, 2002), 444, 334–39.

17. Robert Coram, *Boyd,* 381.

18. Robert Coram, *Boyd,* 374–97; James Kitfield, *Prodigal Soldiers,* 373.

19. James Kitfield, *Prodigal Soldiers,* 209–14.

20. Dana Priest, "Standing Down," *Washington Post,* December 8, 1991, A26.

21. Corissa Jansen and Scott Williams, "Uncle Sam Wants College Graduates," *Milwaukee Journal Sentinel,* March 17, 2003.

22. Arnold Abrams, "More Want Uncle Sam," *Newsday,* July 28, 2003, A2.

23. Charles Moskos and John Sibley Butler, *All That We Can Be* (New York: Basic Books, 1997).

24. James Locher, *Victory on the Potomac* (College Station: Texas A&M University Press, 2002); James Locher, "Has It Worked? The Goldwater-Nicholas Reorganization Act," *Naval War College Review,* October 2001.

25. James Locher, "Has It Worked? The Goldwater-Nichols Reorganization Act," quoting James H. Kyle, *The Guts to Try* (New York: Orion Books, 1990), 283.
26. James Kitfield, *Prodigal Soldiers*, 262.
27. James Kitfield, *Prodigal Soldiers*, 263–68.
28. James Kitfield, *Prodigal Soldiers*, 246–53.
29. Robert Coram, *Boyd*, 425.
30. Robert Coram, *Boyd*, 425.
31. Robert Coram, *Boyd*, 426–27.
32. See Linda Robinson, "The Men in the Shadows," *U.S. News & World Report*, May 19, 2003, 17–20.
33. Fred Kaplan, "*Force Majeure*: What Lies Behind the Military's Victory in Iraq," *Slate*, April 10, 2003.
34. David King and Zachary Karabell, "The Generation of Trust."

CONCLUSION

1. Danielle Crittenden, *amanda bright@home* (New York: Warner, 2003), 1, 6, 34, 42, 18, 20, 21–22.
2. David Brooks, *Bobos in Paradise* (New York: Simon & Schuster, 2000), 10, 52.
3. David Brooks, *Bobos in Paradise*, 52.
4. *Third International Math and Science Study*, 1998, National Center for Education Statistics, cited in Jo Thomas, "Experts Take a Second Look at Virtue of Student Jobs," *New York Times*, May 13, 1998.
5. Ben Wildavsky, "McJobs," *Policy Review*, Summer 1989.
6. *2003 World Almanac*, 264.
7. Ben Wildavsky, "McJobs," *Policy Review*, Summer 1989.

8. John Challenger, "Establishing Rules for the New Workplace," *USA Today,* November 1, 2002.

9. Daniel Pink, *Free Agent Nation* (New York: Warner, 2001).

10. Karlyn Bowman, *Attitudes About Work, Chores, and Leisure in America* (American Enterprise Institute, August 25, 2003), 1–5, 7, 9, 20–21, 41, 30, 63, 66.

11. "America Works," *Wall Street Journal,* August 29, 2003, A8.

12. William Lind et al., "The Changing Face of War: Into the Fourth Generation," *Marine Gazette,* October 1989.

13. William Lind et al., "The Changing Face of War: Into the Fourth Generation," *Marine Gazette,* October 1989.

14. Steven Metz, *Armed Conflict in the 21st Century,* Army War College Strategic Studies Institute, March 2000.

15. William Strauss and Neal Howe, *Millennials Rising* (New York: Random House, 1999).

16. Robert D. Putnam, *Bowling Alone* (New York: Simon & Schuster, 1999).

17. Maggie Gallagher, "Mom's Home—For Good," Townhall.com, June 30, 2003; Kemba Dunham, "Stay-at-Home Dads Fight Stigma," *Wall Street Journal,* August 26, 2003, B1.

18. Brad Todd, "109 Minutes," Instapundit.com, September 16, 2001.

ACKNOWLEDGMENTS

I'm not sure when I started thinking that America has the advanced world's most incompetent eighteen-year-olds and the world's most competent thirty-year-olds, but I think it was on a trip to Britain, when I was impressed with the knowledgeable young people I met there. The obvious conclusion was that we Americans do a lot of things wrong to people between ages six and eighteen and a lot of things right to them between ages eighteen and thirty. In May 2003 I decided to devote my regular column in *U.S. News & World Report* to this theme and in the process of writing it came up with the terms Hard America and Soft America. The column got a good response and seemed to touch a nerve in many people. Some agreed wholeheartedly; some disagreed, partially or vehemently; many had thoughtful things to add. I began to think that there was enough here to be the subject of a book.

The fact that it has become a book so quickly, in just twelve months, is due very much to the efforts of several people, of whom I am only one. My agents, Lynn Chu and Glen Hartley, were enthusiastic about the book and, even more helpful, sent out a proposal and got responses quickly. Steve Ross of Crown Forum responded quickly, and by July I was off and writing. Jed Donahue, who edited my book *The New Americans* for Regnery, had happily moved to Crown Forum in time to edit this book, and once again he provided thoughtful and constructive suggestions and comments. I am grateful, as well, for the careful copy-editing of Margaret Drislane, and for the enthusiasm and energy of everyone else on the Crown Forum team, especially Teresa Brady, Jill Flaxman, and Trisha Howell.

Of the three books I have written and the seventeen *Almanacs of American Politics* of which I have been the principal coauthor, this is the least political and most personal. My ideas have been influenced by literally thousands of relatives, friends, authors, journalists, politicians, academics, and interviewed-on-the-street voters, and I am indebted to all of them—and obviously cannot thank them all by name. But I do want to mention my parents, C. Gerald Barone and Alice Barone, to whom I have been listening, to my great profit, since I was born, and to my sisters and brother-in-law, Marilyn Wagamon and Thomas Wagamon and Patricia Barone, who have taught me more than they probably realize. Thanks also to all the other relatives who debated issues, *McLaughlin Group*–style, around the Thanksgiving and Christmas dinner tables over the years. I also want to thank my colleagues present and past at *U.S. News,* starting but not ending with Mortimer Zuckerman and Brian Duffy, from whom I have learned much at work and in conversation, and my past colleagues at *Reader's Digest,* the *Washington Post,* and Peter D. Hart Research Associates.

Authors almost always say that books are produced only with great agony and over a longer period of time than expected. But I wrote this book on schedule and enjoyed just about every minute of the work. In the process I was prompted to read some wonderful books I had not read before and would probably never have read otherwise— William H. Whyte's *The Organization Man,* Saul Bellow's *Mr. Sammler's Planet,* James Kitfield's *Prodigal Soldiers*—and to consult many wonderful books I had read years ago and would probably not otherwise have returned to.

INDEX

A

Afghanistan, 11–12, 132, 139–40, 153, 157

Agricultural Adjustment Administration (AAA), 28

Aid to Families with Dependent Children (AFDC), 55, 107

Air Force, 133, 135

airline deregulation, 78–79

Allen, Paul, 82

alternative minimum tax, 88

amanda bright@home (Crittenden), 143–46

American Express, 153

American Federation of Teachers, 110

The American High School Today (Conant), 42

apprenticeships, 148

Armstrong, Neil, 45

Army, 128–29, 130, 132, 133, 134, 148

AT&T, 80–81

auto industry, 65–66, 68, 69–70, 112

B

Baker, Russell, 19, 29

Bakke court case, 57

Barbarians at the Gate (Burrough and Helyar), 92–93

Barnes & Noble, 91

Bayh, Evan, 106

Bay of Pigs, 45

Beamer, Lisa, 161

Beamer, Todd, 161

Beatrice Foods, 92

Bellow, Saul, 95–97

Bennett, William, 113

bilingual education, 113–14

blackouts, power, 121–22

Blair, Tony, 117

Bobos in Paradise (Brooks), 145

bonds, high-yield, 90–91, 92

Bowling Alone (Putnam), 159–60

Boyd, John, 133, 138–39, 152, 153

Bradley Foundation, 115

Bratton, William, 100, 102

Brooks, David, 145, 146

Bush, George H. W., 52–53, 114

Bush, George W., 43, 93, 116, 155

C

Cablevision, 91

The Caine Mutiny, 33–34

capital gains tax, 88, 89

Carnegie, Andrew, 22

Caste and Class in a Southern Town (Dollard), 50

Chandler, Raymond, 37–38

charter schools, 116

children. *See also* schools

child labor laws, 23, 29

of "elite" class, 145

generation X, 159

living in poverty, 107

181

children (*cont.*)
millenial generation, 159–60
of single mothers, 103
of stay-at-home parent, 160–61
China, 40–41
CIO unions, 28–29
Civil Aeronautics Board, 78–79
Civil Rights Act, 57
civil rights movement, 47–53, 57
Clinton, Bill, 43, 44, 102, 106,
114, 155
Clinton, Hillary Rodham, 43, 146
Cohen, Eliot, 124–25
Cold War, 40–41, 59
college admissions, 57–58,
111–12, 147–48
Communism, 40–41
community colleges, 111, 147
community policing, 99–100
computers, 82–84
Conant, James, 42
Connor, Eugene "Bull," 50
Council for Basic Education, 114
"creative destruction," 152
crime
criminal justice system, 104,
151–52, 156, 157
increases in, 53–54, 97
link with welfare, 56–57
reducing, 98–102
Crittenden, Danielle, 143

D
Davis, Gray, 81–82
Democracy in America (de
Toqueville), 19
DePuy, William, 131–32
deregulation
electric industry, 81
oil prices, 81
telecommunications industry,
80–81
transportation industry, 77–80

Desert One, 135–36
Detroit riot, 52
Dewey, John, 24–26, 42, 153
Dole, Bob, 106
Dollard, John, 49–50
draft, military, 40–41, 128–29
Dreiser, Theodore, 17–18, 19, 153
Drexel Burnham, 90, 92
drugs, prescription, 156

E
The Economy of Cities (Jacobs),
38–39
education. *See also* schools
bilingual, 113–14
home schooling, 116
progressive, 24–27, 36, 41–42
racial injustice in, 59–60
racial quotas in, 57–58
for veterans, 39–40
Eisenhower, Dwight, 47, 135
electricity deregulation, 81–82
electric power blackouts, 121–22
Elementary and Secondary
Education Act of 1965, 59
Ely, Richard, 22
Energy-Maneuverability theory,
133
Engler, John, 106, 108
English infant schools, 59
Estes, Elliott, 70
European retirement plans, 156
European schools, 146

F
Fair Labor Standards Act, 29–30
FARC, 158
farms, 18, 19, 23
Federal Express, 85, 88
Federal Housing Administration
(FHA), 39, 40
fiscal policy, 72
food stamps program, 55

INDEX

Forstmann, Ted, 116
401(k) plans, 89–90
Friedman, Milton, 115

G

Galbraith, John Kenneth, 32,
    67–68, 71
Gates, Bill, 82–84, 88, 152, 153
GED certificates, 119
General Electric, 86–87, 88
General Motors, 69, 70, 91, 112,
    149
Generation X teenagers, 159
G.I. Bill of Rights, 39–40, 129, 134
Gingrich, Newt, 106
Giuliani, Rudolph, 100–102, 106,
    122, 152, 153
gold standard, 73
Goldwater, Barry, 137
Goldwater-Nichols Act, 137–38
Gore, Al, 43
GPS systems, 139
Gramsci, Antonio, 117
Greene, Harold, 80
The Greening of America (Reich),
    61–63
Greenspan, Alan, 20–21
Grenada, 136–37
Grove, Andy, 82–83
Grutter court case, 58
Gulf War, 132, 138–39, 153

H

Hard America, defined, 13–14
Harrington, Michael, 54
Hasbro, 91
health care, 44, 55, 76, 146, 156
Hirsch, E. D., Jr., 117
HMO regulation, 156
Hoffa, James R., 78
home mortgage guarantees, 39,
    40
home schooling, 116

homework, 109, 147, 159
Honig, Bill, 113
Howe, Neal, 159, 160
Humphrey, Hubert, 57

I

IBM, 82–83, 91
If I Die in a Combat Zone
    (O'Brien), 123–24, 128, 155
illegitimacy rates, 103
The New Industrial State
    (Galbraith), 67–68
inflation, 69, 72, 73
Intel, 82–83
interest income, 88
International Monetary Fund,
    73
Internet browsers, 83–84
Interstate Commerce
    Commission (ICC), 77–78
The Interstate Commerce Omission
    (Nader), 78
IRA, 158
Iraq, 11–12, 140, 153, 157, 158

J

Jacobs, Jane, 38–39
job security, 18–19, 149, 150
Johnson, Lyndon, 45, 52, 124–25,
    126, 127
Johnson, Ross, 92–93
Joint Chiefs of Staff, 135, 137–38
Jones, David, 137
Jones, Reginald, 86
Joyce, Michael, 115
junk bonds, 90–91

K

Kelling, George, 98–100, 102
Kennedy, Edward, 78, 117
Kennedy, John, 45–46, 51, 126
Kennedy, Robert, 55, 78
Kerry, John, 43

INDEX

Keynesian economics, 68, 72–73, 75
King, Martin Luther, Jr., 50–51
Kohlberg Kravis Roberts (KKR), 92–93
Korea, 132
Kravis, Henry, 90, 92–93, 152

L

labor unions
CIO unions, 28–29
declining membership in, 79
legal recognition of, 28
teachers' unions, 110–11, 119–20
Teamsters Union, 77–78
United Auto Workers (UAW), 28–29, 34–35, 69, 110
United Mine Workers, 31, 34–35, 89
United Steelworkers, 28–29, 34–35
during World War II, 30–31
leveraged buyouts, 92–93
Lewis, John L., 31
Lind, William, 157
The Lonely Crowd (Riesman), 33
The Long Goodbye (Chandler), 37–38

M

The Man in the Gray Flannel Suit (Wilson), 34
marijuana, 157
Marines, 130, 133
marriage, 18
McCaw, 91
McDonald's, 147, 149
MCI, 91
McNamara, Robert, 124–25, 127–28
McWhorter, John, 57–58
Medicaid, 55

Medicare, 44, 76
Merrill Lynch, 153
Microsoft, 82–83, 88
military
Air Force, 133, 135
Army, 128–29, 130, 132, 133, 134, 148
corruption in, 128, 130–31
draft, 40–41, 128–29
drug use in, 128, 130, 132
Joint Chiefs of Staff, 135, 137–38
Marines, 130, 133
Navy, 132, 135
public support for, 140–41
race relations in, 134–35
recruitment efforts for, 129–30, 133–34
veterans, benefits for, 39–40
military strategy
in Afghanistan, 11–12, 132, 139–40, 153
Boyd's influence on, 133, 138–39, 152, 153
in Gulf War, 132, 138–39, 153
in Iraq, 11–12, 140, 153
jointness in, establishing, 137–38
jointness in, lack of, 135–37
against terrorism, 157–58
in Vietnam War, 123–29, 131, 135
in World War II, 31–32, 126
Milken, Michael, 90–92, 152
Millenials Rising (Strauss and Howe), 159, 160
Miller, George, 117
Mills, Wilbur, 44
minimum wage, 29–30
Moe, Terry, 120
monetary policy, 72
Morgan, J. P., 20–21, 22
mortgage guarantees, 39, 40

Moynihan, Daniel Patrick, 102–3, 105, 160
Mr. Sammler's Planet (Bellow), 95–97, 155
Murray, Charles, 54, 56–57
Mussolini, Benito, 117

N
Nader, Ralph, 78
NASA, 46
National Assessment of Education Progress (NAEP), 118
National Commission on Excellence in Education, 108
National Council of Teachers of Mathematics, 114
National Defense Education Act, 42
National Education Association (NEA), 110–11
National History Standards, 114
National Recovery Administration (NRA), 28
National Science Foundation, 42
A Nation at Risk, 108, 112
Navy, 132, 135
The Negro Family (Moynihan), 102
Netscape, 83
New Deal legislation, 28–30
News Corporation, 91
New York City, 97, 100–102, 121–22
Nichols, Bill, 137
Nixon, Richard, 44, 69, 73–74, 128
Nunn, Sam, 137

O
O'Brien, Tim, 123–24, 125, 128
oil prices, 81
oil trade, 74
Oldsmobile, 70
OODA Loop, 133

Organization of Petroleum Exporting Countries (OPEC), 74
The Organization Man (Whyte), 33
The Other America (Harrington), 54
overtime pay, 29

P
"Patterns of Conflict," 133, 139
pension plans, 89–90, 157
personal computers, 82–84
Peterson, Paul, 118–19
philanthropy, 22
police officials, 98–102
poverty. *See also* welfare benefits
    children living in, 107
    efforts to reduce, 54–57, 103–4
    link with crime, 55–56
preschool, universal, 156
prescription drug benefits, 156
prison population, 53, 97–98
private-sector economy. *See also* labor unions
    auto industry, 65–66, 68, 69–70, 112
    child labor and, 23, 29
    early 1900s, 20–23, 27–28
    impact of deregulation on, 77–82
    impact of entrepreneurs on, 82–88, 152
    impact of leveraged buyouts on, 90–93
    impact of tax laws on, 89–90
    job satisfaction and, 149–51
    job security and, 18–19, 149, 150
    late 1800s, 18–19, 20
    late 1900s, 75–94, 152
    mid-1900s, 30–36, 38–39, 67–72
    minimum wage and, 29
    space program initiative, 46–47

private-sector economy (*cont.*)
  workmen's compensation and,
    23
  workweek hours and, 23, 29
  during World War II, 30–32
  progressive education, 24–27, 36,
    41–42
Putnam, Robert, 159

Q
Quayle, Dan, 43

R
Rabbit Is Rich (Updike), 65–66,
    155
race relations, in military, 134–35
racial quotas and preferences,
    57–59, 153
racial riots, 51–53
racial segregation, 48–51
railroad deregulation, 79
Rankin, John, 39
Reagan, Ronald, 75, 103
recession, 69
Reich, Charles, 61–63, 66–67
Reich, Robert, 43
retirement benefits
  individual investment accounts
    and, 156–57
  pension plans, 89–90, 157
  Social Security, 29, 35, 44, 76,
    89, 153, 155, 156–57
Reynolds, Glenn, 162
Riesman, David, 33
riots, racial, 51–53
RJR Nabisco, 92–93
robber barons, 20
Rockefeller, John D., 20, 22
Romney, George, 52
Roosevelt, Franklin, 28, 30–32,
    45, 126
Roosevelt, Theodore, 20
Ross, Edward, 22–23

S
Safeway, 92
Scholastic Aptitude Test (SAT)
  scores, 42, 58, 108–9, 118
schools
  academic curriculum at, 26, 27,
    109
  attendance at, 18, 27, 109
  bilingual education at, 113–14
  charter, 116
  college admissions and, 111–12
  innovative teaching methods at,
    113
  mediocrity in, 108–9, 111–12,
    146–47
  national standards for, 114,
    155
  parents' attitudes towards, 111,
    115–16, 158–59
  prior to progressive era, 24
  progressive, 25–27, 36
  public opinions towards,
    158–59
  racial quotas in, 57–58
  in 1800s, 18
  in 1950s, 27
  in 1960s, 42–43, 59–60, 109
  in 1970s, 109
  SAT scores at, 42, 58, 108–9,
    118
  state standards for, 114–15,
    116–18, 154, 158–59
  students' attitudes towards,
    159–60
  students' self-esteem at, 109,
    113
  teachers' unions and, 110–11,
    119–20
  test scores at, 42, 58, 60, 108–9,
    113, 118–19
  universal preschool, 156
  veterans' attendance at,
    39–40

vocational, 148
vocational curriculums at, 26–27
voucher programs for, 115–16, 119
Schumpeter, Joseph, 152
Schwartzkopf, Norman, 136, 139
Sears, 71–72
segregation, 48–51
self-employment, 149
September 11th, 161–62
Shanker, Albert, 110
Shriver, Eunice Kennedy, 154
Simon, William, 92
Sister Carrie (Dreiser), 17–18, 19, 154
Smith, Fred, 84–85, 88
Smith, J. Allen, 23
social connectedness, 36
Social Security, 29, 35, 44, 76, 89, 153, 155, 156–57
Social Security Act, 29, 44
social status, 145–46
Soft America, defined, 13–14
Soros, George, 157
Soviet Union, 40–41, 45
space program, 45–47
Special Olympics, 154
Sperling, John, 148, 157
Sputnik, 41, 42, 45, 152
stagflation, 69, 74–75
Starry, Donn, 131–32
stock market, 28, 88
Strauss, William, 159, 160

T
Talbott, Strobe, 43
taxes, income, 88–89, 155, 156
Taylor, Frederick W., 21–22
Taylorite management, 21–22, 29, 110–11, 130–31, 150
TCI, 91
teachers' unions, 110–11, 119–20

Teamsters Union, 77–78
telecommunications industry, 80–81
Temporary Assistance to Needy Families (TANF), 107
temporary employment, 149
terrorism, 155, 157–58, 161–62
Thompson, Tommy, 105–6, 108, 115, 152
Thurman, Max, 133–34
time-and-motion studies, 21–22, 29
Time Warner, 91, 153
de Toqueville, Alexis, 19
TRADOC (U.S. Army training and doctrine command), 132
Transit Authority of New York, 100–101
transportation industry, 77–80
trucking industry, 77–78
Turner, 91

U
unemployment, 28, 149
unions. *See* labor unions
United Auto Workers (UAW), 28–29, 34–35, 69, 110
United Flight 93, 161–62
United Mine Workers, 31, 34–35, 89
United Steelworkers, 28–29, 34–35
university admissions, 57–58, 111–12, 147–48
University of Phoenix, 148, 157
Updike, John, 65–66
U.S. Air Force, 133, 135
U.S. Army, 128–29, 130, 132, 133, 134, 148
U.S. Marines, 130, 133
U.S. Navy, 132, 135
utilities industry, 81–82

INDEX

V
Veteran Affairs (VA), 39, 40
veterans, 39–40
Viacom, 91
Vietnam Veterans Against the
   War, 43
Vietnam War, 43, 123–29, 131,
   132, 135
vocational schools, 148
Volcker, Paul, 75
voucher programs, 115–16, 119

W
wage and price controls, 73–74
wages, minimum, 29–30
Wagner Act, 28
Wal-Mart, 84, 88
Walton, John, 116
Walton, Sam, 84, 88, 152, 153
Wass de Czege, Huba, 132, 133,
   139
Welch, Jack, 85–87, 88, 152
welfare benefits
   increasing, 54–57, 103–5
   1996 welfare act, 106, 156

restricting, 76, 105–8, 149,
   151–52, 154, 156, 157
work requirements and, 105–8,
   149, 154, 157
Westmoreland, William, 125
Wheless, Hewitt, 31–32
whole language movement, 113
Whyte, William H., 33
Wildavsky, Ben, 147, 149
Williams, Polly, 115
Wilson, James Q., 99, 102
Wilson, Pete, 52
Wilson, Woodrow, 30
workmen's compensation, 23
workweek hours, 23, 29
World Trade Center, 161
World War I, 30
World War II, 30–32, 126, 132
Wyly, Mike, 139

X
X-Prize Foundation, 46–47

Y
Yom Kippur War, 131

ABOUT THE AUTHOR

Michael Barone is a senior writer with *U.S. News & World Report* and a contributor to Fox News Channel. He is the principal coauthor of *The Almanac of American Politics,* published every two years since the 1972 edition, and the author of *Our Country: The Shaping of America from Roosevelt to Reagan* (1990) and *The New Americans: How the Melting Pot Can Work Again* (2001). He grew up in Michigan and graduated from Harvard College and Yale Law School. Barone lives in Washington, D.C.